THE GENESIS OF YOUR GENEALOGY

Step-by-Step Instruction for the Beginner in Family History

Fourth Edition

ELIZABETH L. NICHOLS
Accredited Genealogist

1998

The Genesis of Your Genealogy

© Copyright 1969, 1973, 1992, 1998, Elizabeth L. Nichols. All rights reserved. First edition, 1969. Second edition, 1973; second edition updated, 1981. Third edition, totally revised and enlarged, 1992. Fourth edition, updated and revised, 1998.

No part of this publication in whole or in part may be photographically, mechanically, or electronically copied or transferred without the written consent of the author.

Ancestral File™, Family History Center™, Family History Centers™, Family History Library Catalog™, and SourceGuide™ are trademarks, and FamilySearch®, International Genealogical Index®, and Personal Ancestral File® are registered trademarks of The Church of Jesus Christ of Latter-day Saints and are used with their permission.

Photographs on the cover are of the Harrison H. Nichols family. He is grandfather of the author. Photographs include Harrison in the center, his wife Mabel Louise Farwell, his father, Elijah D. Nichols, two of his daughters, Veva and Leta, and a snapshot of his son Clyde and his wife, Besse (father and mother of the author).

Appreciation: A special thank you to those who have given their encouragement in this work. However, the author takes full responsibility for its content.

Published by
Family History Educators
Box 510606
Salt Lake City, UT 84151-0606

Please note: There is no connection between Family History Educators and the Family History Department of The Church of Jesus Christ of Latter-day Saints.

ISBN: 1-880473-13-5

HOW TO USE THIS BOOK

The first section of this instruction presents some basic information, and then guides you through actions, step by step. By the time you have finished this section, you will not only have learned about the subject, but will have the beginning of your family history recorded on pedigree charts and family group records (on blank forms included).

The second section of this instruction does not contain action assignments. When you have finished reading this section, you will have a basic understanding and mental picture of how computers are used in the field of family history, and can then decide whether to use a computer to find information, to organize and record your information, and to share your genealogical information without needing to retype it.

The third section is a comprehensive glossary that not only defines the terms but also explains them.

The Genesis of Your Genealogy is not new. It has been helping people since 1969. In 1998 this new fourth edition has been updated to the latest computer information.

WHAT IS NEW IN THIS BOOK

This instruction has been updated and enlarged to introduce more fully the topics of:

- using pictures in your family histories
- using the Internet as a family history resource
- additional computer resources now available
- updated illustrations using the latest versions plus more of them

- It has retained its simple introduction to beginning your own family history and to the tools and techniques that you will need, whether you use a piece of paper or a computer.
- It guides you step-by-step in gathering, organizing, and sharing your family history information.
- It assumes that you do not know all of the answers on family history and computers, and gives them to you clearly and simply.
- It includes a section with special helps for the LDS family historian.
- It guides you in handling your data whether you fit into a traditional or blended family.
- It includes both information and ACTION assignments, so that when you have completed the instruction you will have started recording your own family history as well as learned to understand the subject and some basic guidelines for it.
- Its large glossary which both defines and describes enables you to understand what other family historians or instructions are talking about.
- It has been book-club featured.
- It has served more than one university and college class as their required text.
- It has equally served the individual student who wishes to pursue his or her own family history.

CONTENTS

PART ONE: Beginning Your Family History (Step-by-Step) 5

I. Getting acquainted with family history and genealogy 5
   A. What do I need to know to begin? 5
   B. Where will I get the information? 6
   Action: Begin with yourself and what you personally know 6

II. Organizing and recording your information .. 7
   A. Two basic forms 7
   B. How do I fill out these forms? 8
   Action: Write or print your name as no. 1 on a pedigree chart 8
   Action: Fill in the remaining spaces 8
   Action: Use a family group record to list your immediate family group 9

III. Learning about additional sources 10
   A. Personal knowledge of others 10
   Action: Talk to your relatives 10
   B. Sources beyond personal knowledge .. 10
   Action: Gather source material in your home. Study it and carefully extract pertinent genealogical information 11
   C. About specific types of sources 12

IV. Evaluate your information 15
V. Using additional forms and files to organize 16
   A. A research calendar 16
      Action: Begin a research calendar for your family history activities..........17
   B. A calendar of events 17
   C. A document file 17
   D. A discrepancy chart 18
   E. Extend to additional pedigree charts....20
VI. Record sources of information...............20
VII. Helping the LDS family historian..........22
   A. What is different? 22
   B. Family group records 22
   C. Pedigree charts 23
   D. Names for temple ordinances 23
   E. Duplicate checking (for ordinances already done) 25
   F. Computer software programs to record LDS ordinances................26
VIII. Adding to your foundation (More than names).......................................27
   A. Photographs..........................27
   B. Time lines 30
   C. Family heritage 30
      Action: Write down what you know or have heard about your national origins. Write down everything you know, then begin to ask questions.....31
      Action: Write down at least one incident from your own life or that of an ancestor.....................31
IX. Appendices................................31
   A. Major family history organizations....31
   B. Forms..................................33

PART TWO: Computers and Family History/Genealogy 3
I. Learning about computers: an overview ..3
   A. If you've never used a computer......3
   B. Introduction to computers in family history and genealogy 4
II. Using the computer to help you find information....................................4
   A. Library catalogs 4
   B. Genealogical computerized indexes and data files 4
   C. Compact discs........................4
   D. FamilySearch® 4
   E. Electronic media 4
III. Using computers to organize and record your information 4
   A. Equipment you must have............4
   B. Basics of what you will do with any genealogy software program..........5
IV. Using computers to share genealogical information 6
   A. Two ways to share information without retyping it...................6
   B. Many genealogy software programs support GEDCOM 6

PART THREE: Glossary........................6
INDEX 7
Questions with page references for answers 8

PART ONE: BEGINNING *YOUR* FAMILY HISTORY
(STEP-BY-STEP)

I. GETTING ACQUAINTED WITH FAMILY HISTORY AND GENEALOGY

Family history is the identification of the people who make up your family, as many generations back in time (ancestors) and forward in time (descendants) as you choose to include. It also includes glimpses into their lives and the "person" that is represented by the genealogical facts of names, dates, and places for each one.

Family history is something that is shared by all of us, and yet is very unique to each of us.

A. What do I need to know to begin?

To help you identify your family members and their relationships to each other, you need to understand a few basic terms and forms.

- The four parts of identification in family history are
    1. Names
    2. Dates
    3. Places
    4. Relationship (kinship)

These facts form the foundation of genealogy.

- About names

    A person's last name is called a *surname*

    A person's first and middle names are called *given names*.

    The surname of a woman before her marriage is called a *maiden name* or maiden surname.

- About forms

    One way to organize the details of names, dates, places, and relationships is to use forms such as pedigree charts and family group records.

    The pedigree chart serves as a map, showing only direct-line ancestors. It lists the individual and his or her parents, grandparents, great-grandparents, etc.

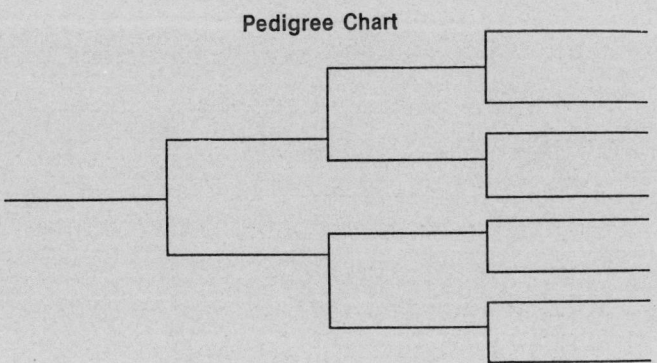

FIRGURE 1- Pedigree chart

Family group records show a father and mother and all of their children, listed in chronological order of birth.

Pedigree charts and family group records can be created on paper, or by using a computer with a genealogical software program designed to organize these facts.

This instruction will cover both methods—paper and computer.

However, it is recommended that you understand basic ways of displaying relationships by listing them on paper before migrating to the computer.

There is no one format of a pedigree chart or family group record. Appendix B shows two sample forms from which to choose. There are many others, and it is simply a matter of one's preference.

While organization in family history is essential, too much organization can take all of your time and may take the fun out of your project. Plan so that you (or anyone else who may study your records) can tell what your system is, and how to find and/or interpret the details and relationships. (If something happens to you, your family would

FIGURE 2- Family group record

want to be able to carry on your family history activities.)

See page 16 for information on other forms, including the research calendar and the calendar of events.

You will have facts that are important but will not have special spaces on the form to record them.

These miscellaneous facts can simply be written on a plain sheet of paper to begin with, and attached to the family group record (or written on the back of the family group record, if there is space), or in the notes section of the computer record. A more organized approach may be considered later.

Some other facts of importance to family history are: occupations, military service, migrations (moves from one place to another), church affiliations, physical descriptions, philosophy of life, sources of the information gathered, and incidents (stories of things that happened).

B. Where will I get the information?

- From personal knowledge of living persons (called oral genealogy)

- From records in your home, the homes of relatives, and of others (called home sources; such as: certificates of birth, marriage, and death, obituaries, announcements, military records, diaries, old letters, pictures, family Bibles, etc.)

- From libraries, courthouses, archives, churches, and cemeteries.

Note: These facilities may house many types of records, including original government-sponsored records of births, marriages, deaths, censuses, and military records; church-created records of christenings (baptisms), weddings, burials; compiled charts and books. All of these may be available on paper, microfilms or microfiche, or in computer data bases. These may be available at libraries or courthouses in your local area.

Action: Begin with yourself and what you personally know.

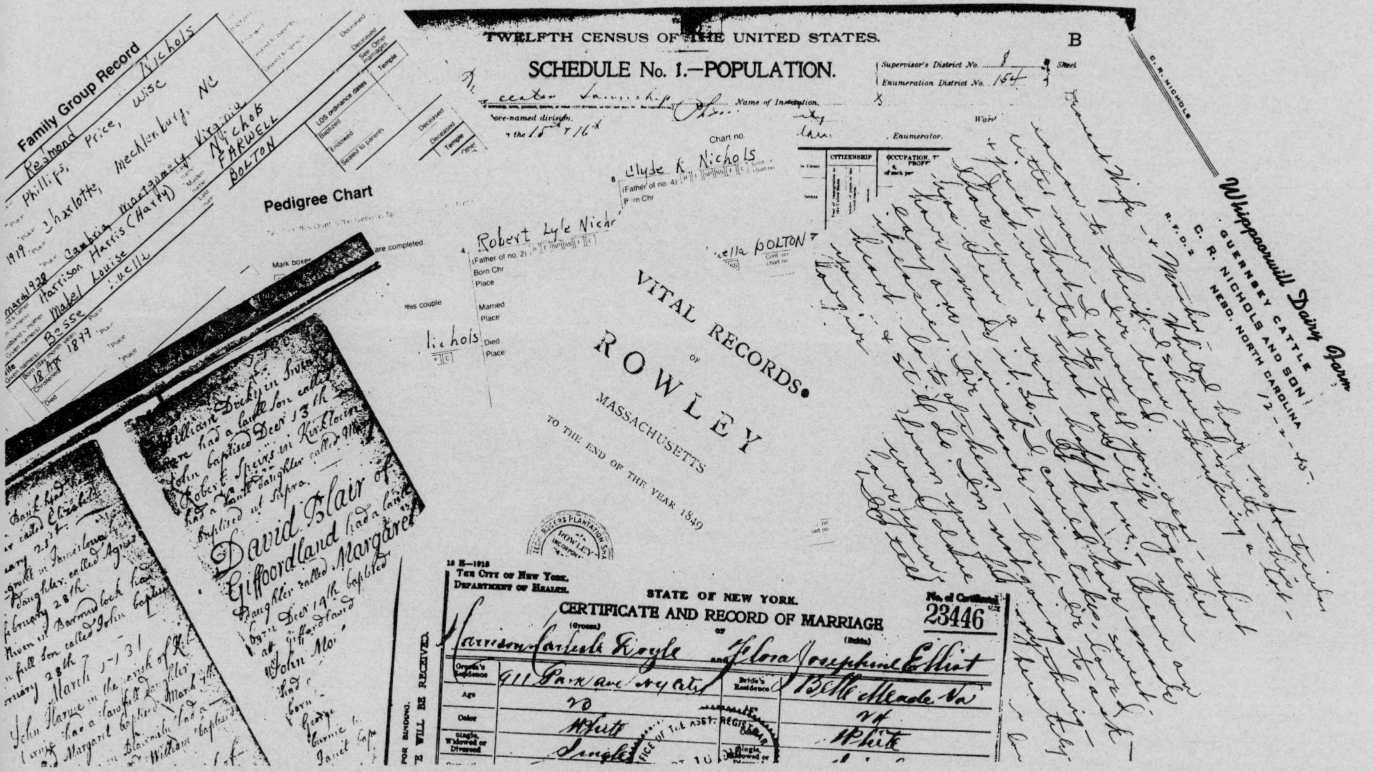

The Genesis of Your Genealogy

FIRGURE 4- Family history sources

II. ORGANIZING AND RECORDING YOUR INFORMATION

A. Two basic forms

There are two basic forms that you will use in organizing family history information:

- *Pedigree charts* outline your relationship to your direct ancestors—that is, to your parents, grandparents, great-grandparents, great-great-grandparents, etc. It serves as your map.

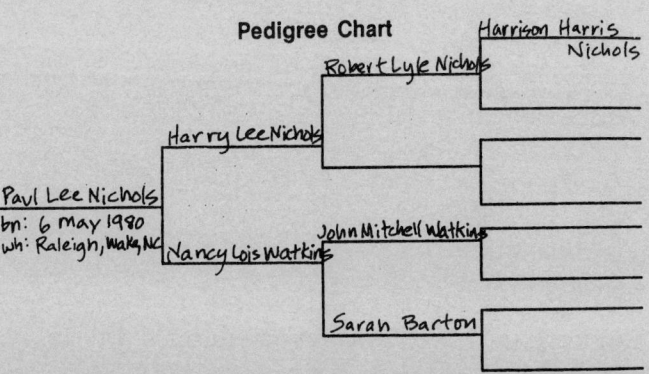

FIGURE 6- A pedigree chart records information about your family

- *Family group records* show a family unit—a father, mother, and all of their children (includes all brothers and sisters of those names appearing on the pedigree chart). Additional family groups can be prepared to record information on additional marriages of ancestors and the children of these families, on your cousins, and other relatives.)

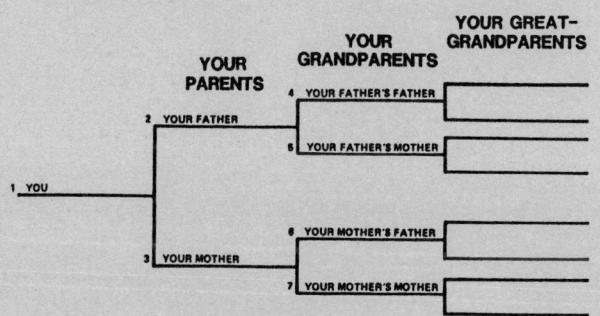

FIGURE 5- A pedigree chart showing relationships

These forms in some format will usually be available from your local genealogical society or

7

The Genesis of Your Genealogy

Family Group Record	Page / of /
Husband's name (first middle last)	Harry Lee Nichols
Born (day month year)	13 Nov 1952	Place	Ogden, Weber, Utah
Chr.		Place	
Marr. 27 May 1978	Place	Kensington, Maryland
Died		Place	
Bur.		Place	
Husband's father's name (first middle last)	Robert Lyle Nichols
Husband's mother's maiden name (first middle last)	Dorothy Dutton
Wife's maiden name (first middle last)	Nancy Lois Watkins
Born (day month year) 22 Feb 1956	Place	Chase City, Mecklenburg, VA
Chr.		Place	
Died		Place	
Bur.		Place	
Wife's father's name (first middle last)	John Mitchell Watkins
Wife's mother's maiden name (first middle last)	Sarah Barton
Children — List each child (whether living or dead) in order of birth.	
1. Name (first middle last)	Paul Lee Nichols
Sex M — Born (day month year) 6 May 1980	Place	Raleigh, Wake, NC
Chr.		Place	
Died		Place	
Spouse name (first middle last)	
Marr.		Place	
2. Name (first middle last)	Sarah Melissa Nichols
Sex F — Born (day month year) 2 Feb 1982	Place	Spartanburg, Spartanburg, SC
Chr.		Place	
Died		Place	
Spouse name (first middle last)	
Marr.		Place	

FIGURE 7- *A family group record includes information on a family unit*

library, or from a genealogical supply store near you. They are also available through many mail order services.

The pedigree chart and family group record form, in some format, can never become outdated, because the relationships outlined on these forms—parents and children from generation to generation—are essential to the identification of individuals as members of *your* family.

However, formats do vary, and there are many from which you can choose. The ones used in this book are available from the LDS Church or the family history center in your area; or from Everton Publishers, P. O. Box 368, Logan, UT 84321. Everton will send a free catalog of genealogical supplies, upon request.

B. How do I fill out these forms?

Action: Write or print your name as no. 1 on a pedigree chart.

- Recording names

  Write the name as you speak it—given name, middle name, and surname (last name). You may want to write the last name in all capital letters:

  Harrison Harris (Harry) NICHOLS

  Effie Mae DEWEESE

  Hendrick VAN DER WEKKEN

  Robert "N" DUTTON (No name, but just an initial)

  Write your father's name as number 2 on the chart, and your mother's name as number 3. Use your mother's maiden surname (as it was before she was married). For example, the wife of Harrison Nichols would be listed as

  Mabel Louise FARWELL

- Recording dates

  Go back to your name, and add your birth date. Write it in the military style—day, month, and year. Write the abbreviation of the month. Do not use numbers for the month, because they can be confusing. Use all four digits to write the year.

  26 May 1937

  7 Sep 1859

- Recording places

  Add the place of your birth. Include town, county, and state (or equivalents). Record the smallest level first.

  Then record the dates and places for your parents.

  Examples:

  Starks, Somerset, Maine
  Lynn, Essex, MA
  Newside Parish, Dalry, Ayr, Scotland
  Sharon Memorial Gardens Cemetery, Charlotte, Mecklenburg, North Carolina

Action: Fill in the remaining spaces.

Add the names of your grandparents. Your father's father is number 4 and his mother is number 5 on the pedigree chart; your mother's father is number 6, and her mother is number 7. Can you see how the chart is organized? Even numbers are always fathers; uneven numbers are always mothers. And they always link to their child. It is easy to see where each name goes.

When you have more names than will fit on one pedigree chart, you will want to continue them on additional charts. See page 20 for how to do this.

Add all the names, dates, and places to your chart that you know. Leave spaces to fill in the information you do not know.

You may want to write in pencil, especially the information you need to check on for spelling or other facts.

This is your work chart. It does not matter if you make mistakes and have to correct them.

This foundation is needed whether you plan to record your family genealogy on paper or use a computer.

Important Note: Even if you are going to use a computer, you need to understand the organization of the information on pedigree charts and family groups. Therefore, it is recommended that you fill out your first pedigree chart and two family group forms—one where you are spouse (parent) and one where you are a child.

Action: Now take a family group record and fill it out for your immediate family.

- Filling in the forms
  1. If you are married, put the husband on the first line; if you are single, go to step four and begin with your father.
  2. Add the name of the wife, and then the names of the children, beginning with the oldest child.
  3. Be sure to indicate the sex of each child, by placing either an F or M in the column labeled sex.
  4. Next, make out another family group record—where you are a child, listing your parents, and brothers and sisters with you on the form.
  5. Place an X beside your name—so you can quickly identify the person of greatest interest to you. On the family groups where your parents are listed as children, place an X beside the name of your direct ancestor(s).
  6. If a person was married more than once, there should be a separate family group form prepared for each marriage, listing the spouse and children for that marriage.

     Names of additional spouses with the dates of marriage are usually listed on the back of each family group record form. Divorces may also be listed there, where appropriate.
  7. You may also indicate a divorce for a marriage listed on the family group record by writing the letters DIV following the marriage date.

- Recording blended families

  If you choose, list adopted, step-brothers or -sisters, and\or half-brothers and -sisters all on the same form. You may want to indicate in the notes the blood relationships of the various members of your family.

  Where you feel close to both a step or adopted parent and to a bloodline parent, you may want to prepare your pedigree chart showing the parents you usually list in other records, and then prepare an additional pedigree chart beginning with the other parent.

  For example, if Mary Brown was born the child of John Brown and Susan Smith, but raised by her mother Susan Smith, and Susan's second husband, William Jones, you may want to show Mary Brown on the same family group record with the other children of William Jones and Susan Smith. The pedigree chart may show Mary's parents as William Jones and Susan Smith. An additional pedigree chart may begin with the name of John Brown, and show his ancestors.

Or you may wish to show the parents on the pedigree chart as John Brown and Susan Smith, and prepare a second pedigree chart beginning with William Jones.

Be sensitive to the feelings of all concerned. You cannot always please everyone, and sometimes must accept that fact. But people are more important than forms or procedures.

Note: Doing family history or genealogical research is exactly the same for members of The Church of Jesus Christ of Latter-day Saints (LDS, Mormons) and those who are not members However, the purposes for which one does research may vary. Members of the LDS Church have additional tasks to do and details to record. For Special Helps for members of The Church of Jesus Christ of Latter-day Saints, see page 22.

III. LEARNING ABOUT ADDITIONAL SOURCES

A. Personal knowledge of others

- Extend next to the personal knowledge and memories of other members of your family—parents, brothers and sisters, cousins, uncles, aunts, grandparents, great-grandparents—anyone who is alive who might know the facts that will help you fill in the blanks on your charts.

- Realize that your own brothers and sisters may know things that you don't. It may surprise you what they were interested in and remember. And when you put your facts together, you may have much more information than you do alone. For example, one sister knew that a grandmother's maiden name was BRIM. An older sister knew that the original spelling was BREHM—which can make a big difference in tracing the individual and family.

Action: Talk to your relatives, and see what information they can add about your family members.

- Be sure to have a paper and sharp pencil or pen with you when you talk to them—in your home, by visit or by telephone. Or you may want to take a tape recorder and record the conversation (with permission, of course).

- It is helpful if you have your forms with you, or have written down specific things you want to learn, such as "what is Grandma's maiden surname?" "did Grandpa serve in the army?" or "where was Aunt Veva born?"

- Write to those you cannot visit or telephone. Enclose a stamped, self-addressed envelope for their convenience.

- You may find other distant relatives by placing queries in genealogical periodicals, and/or by studying those placed by others.

- *In summary,* you need to recall the information you know, then communicate with relatives about your desire to locate family history information, investigate possible sources, and advertise to reach beyond known relatives.

B. Sources beyond personal knowledge

Personal knowledge is priceless, but records are usually needed to verify the older facts and to extend beyond what anyone now living may know.

- *Begin in your home,* and see what records you may have that will help in your family history project.

    Items to look for include certificates of birth, marriage, death, church baptism, confirmation, announcements of births and marriages, funeral programs and obituaries, military discharge papers, newspaper clippings, diaries, journals, old letters, scraps of paper with family information carefully recorded on them (check the family Bible—it often contains treasured bits of information written down and placed there for safe-keeping), land deeds, pedigree charts, family group records, printed histories and genealogies, etc, etc.

Action: Gather together the papers and documents that you find in your home. Carefully study them, and extract each bit of information that may be helpful to you.

You will need to go through these records several times. You will miss many things the first time or two you read them.

- Extend to homes of relatives

Living family members do not have to be close to you either in locality or in your life. Locate them, and then ask them questions about your family heritage. They are usually very happy to assist you.

You may visit them in person, write them a letter, or call them on the telephone.

1. Be kind, courteous of their time and needs, organized, and brief—unless they invite you to be otherwise.

2. If you are planning a visit, it is usually best to phone or write first. This will allow them to be thinking about what you want to discuss. You can then make an appointment so they will have time to spend with you.

3. Letters are often best answered if they arrive on Friday, so they can be answered on the weekend. (They may be forgotten if they arrive on Monday,

FIGURE 8- Family history resources

and there is no time to consider them until the next weekend.)

4. If you are making a telephone call, ask the person if this is a convenient time to talk, or if you should call back later.

5. Have your materials organized and available to you at the phone, and a pencil and paper to write down notes on the facts you are given.

6. Ask relatives to look for the records in their homes and the homes of their close relatives for anything that will tell you about your family.

7. Like the rest of us, you have many relatives that you do not know, but who may have the information you are seeking.

8. If the relative who has the information you are seeking is one whom you do not know, there are several ways to locate such information. One of them is Ancestral File (see page 44). Another is to place or respond to queries listed in genealogical periodicals and newsletters. There are many of these from which to choose—some international in scope, some national, some regional, and some local to a particular state or county. Libraries can often help you identify periodicals from which to choose.

One of the largest of U.S. national scope is Everton's *Genealogical Helper* (Logan, Utah: Everton Publishers). The genealogical section of your local library, or a local genealogical library, may have a copy that you can review.

If you begin with one couple and they have four children, and each of those four have four children, in four generations you have 256 direct descendants; in ten generations you have one million descendants.

If each person were to have individual and distinct ancestry back to the year 1050, you have a total of 134 million progenitors. But in the year 1050, in England, the total population was only 1.25 million people. We are all members of the same family—and tracing our ancestry only confirms this.

- Visit or write facilities that may have helpful information

1. If you live in the locality where your ancestors have lived for some time (or if you can visit such a place), then go to the cemetery where your family members are buried. Cemeteries have two types of records: tombstones and office records, called sexton's records.

2. The local genealogical or public library near where they are buried will probably have copies of newspapers, where you can find obituaries and possibly other interesting items, once you have the names and dates to look for.

3. Letters to libraries are a possibility if you live far away. Organize your questions so the facts are briefly stated and it is clear what you want them to look for. Limit your questions to one or two per letter, and include at least a stamped, self-addressed envelope (and usually a couple of dollars with your request). Many libraries will look in indexes for you for one item—but none can do extensive research for you free of charge.

4. Churches where your ancestors and their families attended usually will have created records of baptism, confirmation, weddings, burials, and sometimes transfers to other congregations.

5. County courthouses, archives, or state and city offices of vital statistics may have records that can help you. (There may be a charge for these records.)

C. About specific types of sources

There are many other sources you can and will use. Among the major ones will be:

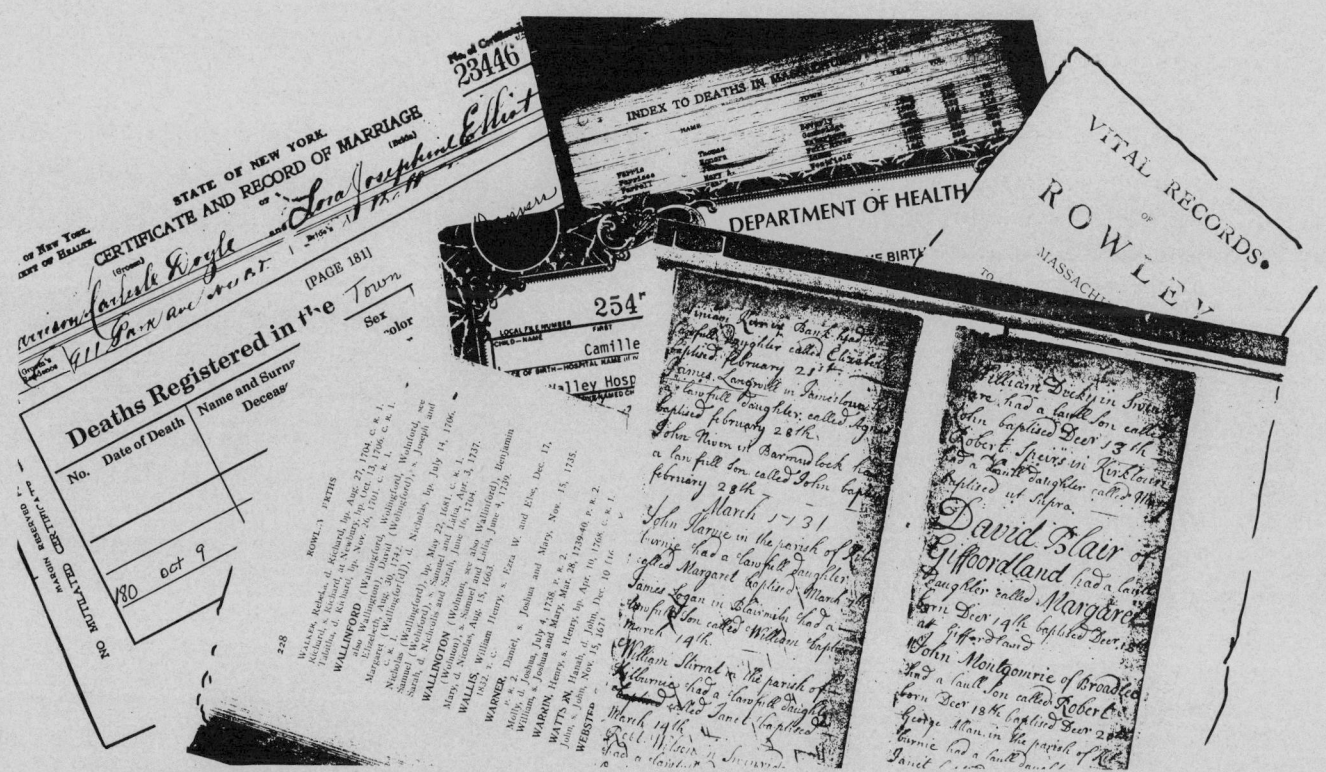

FIGURE 9- *Vital records include certificates and courthouse records—and printed or microfilmed copies of these*

- Records of births, marriages, and/or deaths, recorded by governments

These may be found in offices of town or city clerks, county courthouses, or stored in state archives or libraries; copies of them may be available in your local libraries.

Records for modern time periods (where the people listed in them may still be living) are usually restricted to access by close family members.

Records in county courthouses will include the births, marriages, and deaths/burials that occurred in their areas for certain time periods. These records created by governments are known by different terms in different countries. In the United States and Canada, they are called vital records; in most other countries they are called civil registration.

If you can visit the county courthouse which served your family, you can often find the vital records for older generations.

For information on where to find these U.S. records, consult the pamphlet "Where to Write for Vital Records" (Washington, D.C.: U.S. Department of Health and Human Services), available in many libraries or from the U.S. Government Printing Office for a small fee, currently known as item no. 017-002-01196-4. Call them at 202-512-1800; or order from consumer information catalog at www.pueblo.gsa.gov (item 127E).

You can sometimes find this pamphlet in genealogical bookstores. Or you may request a single copy from the government printing office.

To determine if copies of birth, marriage, and death records are available, check the library catalog of the genealogical and public libraries near you. They may have many of the earlier records on microfilm.

The Family History Library in Salt Lake City, Utah and its 2,000 family history centers (branches) scattered throughout the world make access to many of these records available to anyone for research purposes without charge for the facilities.

- Census records

Census records are enumerations of the population of a country, often for the purposes of determining its military strength. Beginning in the mid-1800s (1841 in some countries, like England and Canada; 1850 in the United States) federal census records began to list by name all members of a family living within the household at that time, and include their age and state or country of birth. Beginning with the 1880 census, it included the relationship to the head of the household for each person listed, and the state or country of birth for the father and mother of each person listed.

(Unfortunately, the 1890 U.S. census was destroyed, except for a few miscellaneous counties, and a portion of a special listing of civil war veterans or their widows.)

Census records are usually indexed, making it easy to find your family if you know the state (or equivalent) where your family was living when a major census was taken (each ten years in most countries).

The latest U.S. census to be released is the 1920 census, released in 1992 (72 years after the census was taken, to protect the privacy of citizens listed).

There may also be state or other localized census records—often taken in years between federal census records.

Census records for your area, on microfilm, are often easily available through libraries. If the library does not have them, they may be borrowed for you by the library. Check with your librarian.

- There are also many records already compiled into family groups and/or pedigrees. These may be found in your

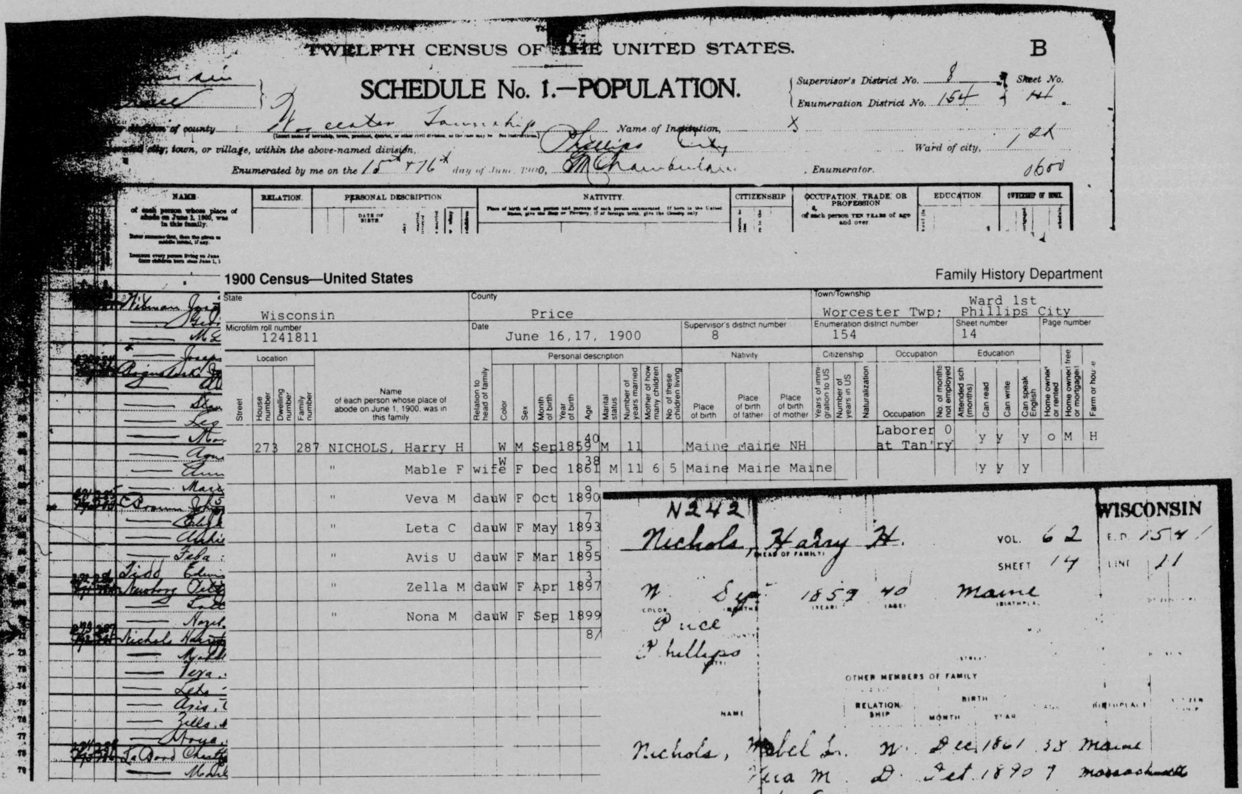

FIGURE 10- U. S. census records

FIGURE 11- A roll of microfilm

own families—in charts or books. Or they may be in libraries. They may be in book form, or on microfilm or microfiche, or in computer data bases.

See page 41 for more information.

- Maps and gazetteers will help you understand the relationship of one place to another. Remember that boundaries may have changed, and consider what the map looked like at the time of the events you are interested in.

More information about genealogical sources is available in many reference books and articles. If your research is in the United States, an excellent one is *The Researcher's Guide to American Genealogy* by Val D. Greenwood, 2nd edition (Baltimore: Genealogical Publishing Co., 1990). For research in other counties, consult with your local library or genealogical society. There are many how-to books for each area.

IV. EVALUATING YOUR INFORMATION

You will need to carefully consider the various facts and inferences you receive in your family history research. The statement that all truth is not of the same value applies in family history. And the way truths are put together can sometimes result in false assumptions.

For example, if you have a record for the marriage of Harry Nichols and Mabel Cook in 1881 in your area, and you have a 1900 census showing Harry Nichols with wife Mabel and six children, you may think the record is providing evidence that this is the same couple. However, more careful search of all records will reveal a death record for the first Mrs. Mabel Cook Nichols, and a second marriage for Harry to Mabel Farwell. Further research will reveal that both of the children born to Mabel Cook and Harry Nichols died as children. Therefore, if you are a descendant of Harry and Mabel and you trace the ancestry of Mabel Cook, you are on the wrong line! The mother of your ancestor was Mabel Farwell.

If analysis is omitted or poorly done, the entire project is unstable. Of particular importance is proving the links from one generation to another. (Remember there are almost always several people with the same name; you must identify the records that pertain to *your* Mabel Nichols.)

Comparing ages for the ancestor in the various records will often help. For example, if your ancestor was named Abigail Howe, whose child was born in 1819, and you find an Abigail How in the right place born in 1795, you may think she is yours (and she may be). But continue to look. If you then find the marriage record of your ancestor, where Abigail Howe married John Doe, they were married in 1806, you have a problem (she would have been only 11 years old). If the census records, and her death record all agree that she was born about 1790, you have the wrong Abigail Howe in

FIGURE 12- Books, microfiche, microfilm, and computer all may be useful to the family historian

RESEARCH CALENDAR   P. 1

Ancestor's name: Harrison H. Nichols

Objective(s): Identify him & find out how many children he had

Locality: Maine, Mass, Wisc

Date of search	Location/ call number	Description of source (Author, title, year, pages)	Comments (Purpose of search, results, years and names searched)	Doc. number
6/1992	In person	Talked to Mom & Grandpa Nichols	To see what they knew	N-1
6/92	Home	gathered obituaries, newspaper clippings, pictures, old letters, certificates	To see what information these records have	N-2 A-
6/92	International Genealogical Index (IGI)	H. H. Nichols 1992 ed on compact disc	To find marriages, children, Bros. & Sis. Found 2 children	N-3
6/92	Ancestral File	H. H. Nichols & families	Families & pedigree; children by 1st marriage estimated dates only	N-4
7/92	FHL film 1249538	1900 US Soundex (N-242)	listed 5 children	N-5

FIGURE 13- *A research calendar*

the one born in 1795. Keep looking—even though you don't seem to find anything for a long time.

The important thing is first to gather everything you can, and then to evaluate it. Become a family detective, and apply the guidelines of investigation and evaluation of both facts and evidence. And enjoy the process. It can be fun; it can be a great source of recreation; and it can sometimes challenge you to find and document the truth. But such challenges can be refreshing and rewarding.

V. USING ADDITIONAL FORMS AND FILES TO ORGANIZE

A. A Research Calendar

This is an outline of your activities, and should include all types of sources—including "talked to Mom," "gathered the documents in my home," or "studied the 1910 U.S. census for Ladysmith, Rusk County, Wisconsin for the Harrison Harris Nichols family" (at the local LDS family history center, FHL film no. 1020981, page 172, document N-10).

The research calendar details what sources you use (or plan to use), along with the method (telephone, correspondence with whom—including the address, library call number, etc.), what you were looking for, what your results were, reference to any copies of documents or extended notes that you made, and the date of the search.

When you have identified a question you want answered, you can make an entry on your research calendar, if you wish. For example, "find the marriage date of Great-Grandpa A. E. Bolton" or "find the maiden surname of his wife."

Your research calendar (sometimes called a log) can contain a summary of the records you have already searched, and an outline of those you plan to search. As such, it can serve as a work outline for the future as well as a history of what you have done.

Calendar of Events HARRISON HARRIS (HARRY) NICHOLS

WHEN	WHAT	WHERE
1859 Sept	Born	Starks, Somerset, Maine
1881	Married	? to Mabel Cook
1880s	children born	probably Massachusetts
1880s	deaths of wife & daughter	" "
1889 Oct	re-married	Lynn, Essex, MA to Mabel Louise FARWELL
1890-93	children born	Massachusetts
1890s	son died (2 sons)	probably MA; or WI
1895-1902	children born	Wisconsin
abt 1911	Town burned down	Buswell, WI a lumber town where he was foreman; families evacuated to an island
abt 1912	moved	Ladysmith, Rusk, Wisc
abt 1935	broke his hip	?
?	leg amputated	
1939 Oct	Golden Wedding Anniversary	Ladysmith, Wisc had children living in Wisc, Mich, Ind, NC

FIGURE 14- Calendar of Events

Action: Begin a research calendar for your family research activities.

B. A Calendar of Events

This serves to organize the events in the life of an ancestor. It outlines *when, what, where*. This allows you to write the story of someone's life, or to know where to look for records of birth, marriage, death, census, military, land, church, or other items telling about that person or family.

C. A document file

This is a file where you keep documents (birth certificates, obituaries, wedding notices, etc.), notes made from documents, or copies of documents (such as a photocopy of the 1910 census showing your family). It can be manila envelopes in a box under the bed, a binder with envelopes to hold the documents, or a drawer in a filing cabinet. But it should be organized and cared for.

Your research calendar, family group record sources, and notes will refer to the document file. You may use numbers, surnames, or initials plus numbers (or any other system that suits you) to identify your documents. For example, your Nichols documents may be prefixed with the letter N, and if you have several obituaries pertaining to one family, you may want to number them all N-8, and have letters refer to the individual obituaries, such as N-8-a, N-8-b.)

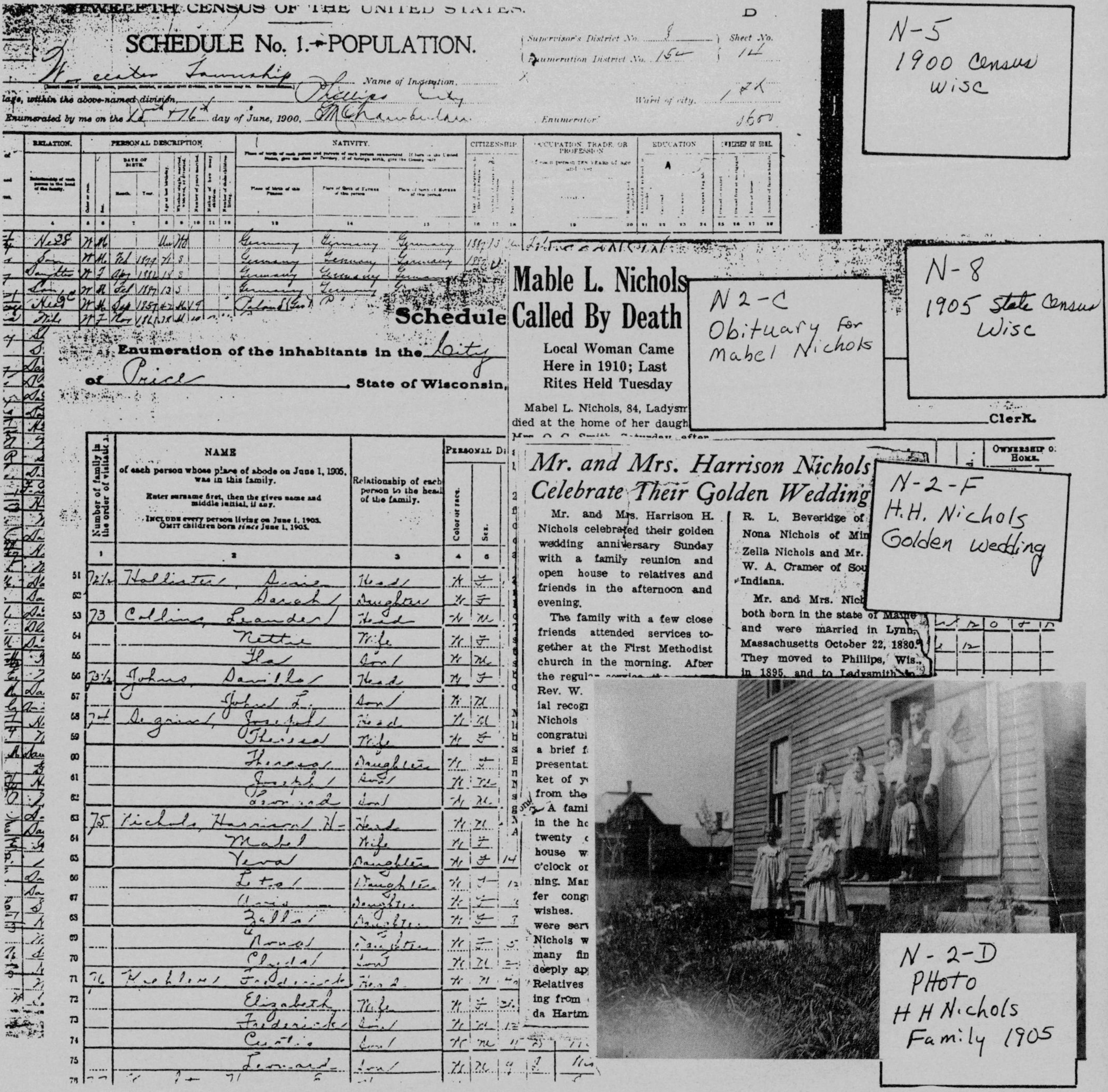

The Genesis of Your Genealogy

FIGURE 15- *Documents may be identified with numbers*

D. A Discrepancy Chart

It will be natural in your family history research to receive conflicting information about the same events. For example, you may find a record of marriage that says Jean was age 22, when the census taken two years earlier says she was then 25; or you may find a person's name written as Annie one time and Mary next time and Mary Anne the next time—yet they may all refer to the same person. Or a man may go by a middle name during childhood and youth, and then begin using his first name—especially if his first name is the same as his father's. Yet these discrepancies in names—that is, in the words we use to describe a person—may all refer to the same person.

Study the details of all versions of information with their sources. Determine whether different records are referring to the same person with varied details

18

DISCREPANCY CHART

Record	Name	Date of Birth	Place of Birth	Date of Marriage	Place of Marriage	Parents
Census, 1860	Harrison	[1859] (age 8 mo)	Maine			Elijah D. Nichols, Betsy A.
1900	Harry	1859 (age 40)	Maine			—
1905	Harrison	[1859] (age 45)	Maine			—
Marriage Record	Harry			2nd - 1889 to Mabel Farwell	Lynn, Mass	
Death Record	Harrison	1859 (age 80)	Maine			Elijah & Betsy Nichols
I.G.I. 1988 Batch Nos. H---, 78---, A---	Harrison, as father of his children	—	—	22 Oct 1889	Lynn, Essex, MA	
Ancestral File 1991 ed	Harrison Harris or Harry	1859	Maine	1881 - 1st, 1889 - 2nd	MA, Lynn, MA	Elijah D, Betsey Ann
Family Bible	Harrison	1859	—	1889	—	— listed him as parent

FIGURE 16 - A discrepancy chart

identifying him/her, or if the records are referring to two (or more) persons with similar identifying information. *A failure to do this type of analysis when you get beyond personal knowledge can cause you to create false links and trace the wrong family lines.*

One way to display this information for review and study is to create a chart. Take the records that you think pertain to your ancestor and list them down the side of the page. Next take the element (birth date, name of parents) and list it next to the source, across the page. Then write in the information from each source.

You may want to do this for each event or name, and then put them together.

This type of discrepancy chart is explained in more detail in *Genealogical Research Standards* by Derek Harland, published in 1963.)

You could compare as few or as many elements as you wish.

A comparison of names of a spouse may also be helpful.

But remember, a woman's name may be listed several ways due to one or more marriages. She would be married the first time under her maiden surname, but a second time under the surname of her first husband. (You may find her first marriage by tracing that surname, but you won't find her parents with that surname [unless her maiden surname was the same, which does happen but is unusual]. You must find her maiden surname to identify her parents.) The middle name or initial she uses may refer to her maiden surname, or to a middle given name.

The number of children in a family is another item that you may want to chart. Often one or more died in childhood, and will be missed unless you are careful.

By charting the discrepancies, you can study the facts and evidence in each record, and see which elements match and where there are differences.

E. Extend to additional pedigree charts

When you have more generations than will fit on one pedigree chart, you will need to begin a second one—and then a third one, etc.

The key to using these charts successfully is simple: cross-reference each one to the other.

If you are working with a four-generation pedigree chart, the name of your paternal great-grandfather is no. 8 on chart no. 1. It has a little line after the name, where it may say "this name is continued on chart no___."

When you are ready to extend this pedigree, you can place a 2 there. On a blank pedigree chart, place a 2 at the top of the form where it says "Chart no." Then look in the left-hand corner of the chart where it says "name no. 1 on this chart is the same as name no. ___ on chart no. ___." In this case, you would say name no. 8 on chart no. 1.

His wife's ancestors may be listed on pedigree chart no. 3, and the cross-reference would read "this person is the same as person no. 9 on chart no. 1."

If you are working with a five-generation chart, the name you continue is no. 16 for your paternal great-great-grandfather, and no. 17 for his wife. (See page 32.)

If you are continuing the ancestry of your maternal grandfather, he would be the same person as number 12 on a four-generation chart (or number 24 on a five-generation chart).

VI. RECORDING SOURCES OF INFORMATION

Recording the sources of your information is very important, but need not be elaborate.

If your source of the birth date for Grandpa Nichols is "personal knowledge of his daughter, Avis Nichols Smith, recorded in 1953 in a letter to her brother," write that down; if your source is the "Cemetery record of Memorial Gardens, Charlotte, Mecklenburg, NC," state that; if your source is "obituary of Clyde R. Nichols, Sr.," write it down.

It is best if you are specific to each basic fact. And this can be done in a variety of ways. You may want to list your sources, with either letters or numbers, and then refer to these in documenting each fact:

You can give an identification letter or number to each specific source, such as:

A. Marriage record of Harry Nichols and Mabel Louise Farwell
    Copy of marriage certificate from state of MA, in possession of Elizabeth L. Nichols

B. 1905 state census of Wisconsin (Phillips, Price County), page 172 (FHL film 1020981), showing Harry as a parent

C. 1900 US federal census soundex of WI (soundex code N242, FHL film no. 1249538; actual census—Ladysmith, Rusk County, page 00 (FHL film 1241811), showing Harry as a parent

D. Family Bible record where Harrison Nichols is a parent

E. Obituaries

F. Golden wedding anniversary celebration announcement for Harry and Mabel Farwell Nichols

G. 1860 census of Starks, Somerset County, Maine, for the family of Elijah D Nichols (where Harrison is a child, age 8 months), typed page 13 (handwritten page 153); FHL film 803452)

H. Birth certificates

I. Cemetery records copied in 1953 by Veva Nichols Cramer (dau of Harrison) and her personal knowledge recorded in 1953

J. Ancestral File, 1990 edition (See page 00)

K. International Genealogical Index, 1988 edition (See page 00)

BIRTHS: Husband: G, E, B, C, I, J
Wife: F, B, C, I, J
Child #1: H, D, I, J, K
Child #2 D, I, J
Child #3 H (MA), D, J (batch no. 83000-61)
Marriages:
Husband & wife: A, F, J
child #1 I (her own statement), J

The Genesis of Your Genealogy

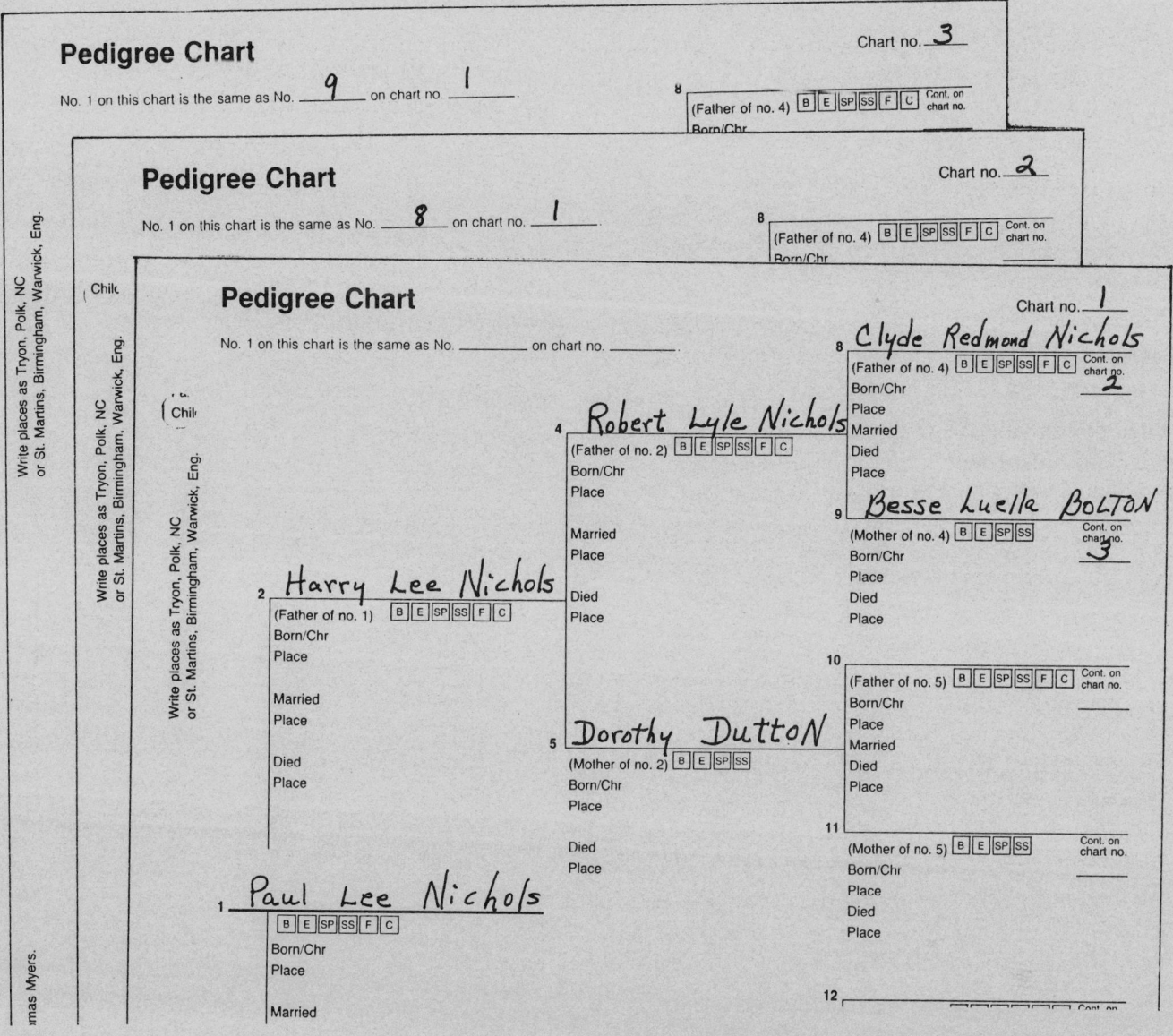

FIGURE 17- *Pedigree charts are cross-referenced*

Such a detailed record will allow you to always know your source of any specific information. This becomes important if you find conflicting information, which is always the case in family history research.

For example, if Cousin Jane calls you and tells you that she has the marriage record of Grandpa Harry Nichols, and his name was not Harrison—it was Harry—you can check your sources and see that you have him listed in the 1860 census of Maine, when he would have been only a baby. You can go to your research calendar, see what the document number is, and check that record—the earliest record you have. It lists his name as Harrison—as does the 1905 census record where he is a parent, and his obituary. However, the 1910 census lists him as Harry. You can tell Cousin Jane the sources of your information. And you can both realize that he sometimes wrote his name as Harry, while at other times he used the formal name of Harrison. Both names refer to the same individual.

Note: There are many ways you can keep your source notes. The important thing is for you to keep them. There are books and articles available to help you.

(See also page 53 for possible ways to keep source citations in a genealogy computer program, such as Personal Ancestral File.)

21

VII. HELPING THE LDS FAMILY HISTORIAN

A. What is different?

Doing family history or genealogical research is exactly the same for both members and those who are not members of The Church of Jesus Christ of Latter-day Saints (LDS, Mormons). However, the purposes for which one does research may vary.

Members of the LDS Church have additional tasks to perform and details to keep tract of.

Once you have identified your family members, you want to know whether or not they have already received the ordinances of the gospel of Jesus Christ as administered through the authority of the priesthood of God. There are four ordinances that you want to record: LDS baptism, endowment, sealing to spouse, and sealing of child to parents (may be BIC for Born in the Covenant, if the child was born after the parents were sealed as a couple in an LDS temple). These ordinances may have been received personally during the lifetime of the person, or by proxy after the death of the individual (in which case the person has the choice to accept or reject the ordinances in the spirit world where he or she now resides). The Lord will make the final judgment on a person's worthiness.

B. Family group records

There are spaces on the LDS-published family group record forms to record the dates for these ordinances, and the temple where each was performed. (LDS baptisms for the living do not need to be performed in a temple. The word LIVE or LIV can be written or typed in the temple space for baptisms performed during the lifetime of the person.)

The abbreviations used as labels for these ordinances are:

B: = LDS baptism

E: = endowment

SP: = sealed to parents

SS: = sealed to spouse

Caution: Different versions of family group record forms have these blanks in different order on the form. *Be careful not to record the sealing to spouse in the sealing to parents space on the form.*

Newer forms have a different arrangement of data—listing the birth, christening, death, burial, and then the marriage date. This allows the baptism, endowment, and sealing to parents dates to be listed together on the form, as they are in the Ordinance Index (main file and Addendum), followed by the sealing to spouse, which can then be listed directly across from the marriage date and place on the form.

See the blank form on page 35.

Note: The christening date is baptism into any

LDS ordinance dates	Temple
Baptized	
Endowed	
Sealed to parents	
Sealed to spouse	

FIGURE 18- LDS ordinance boxes

other religion. (It is *not* an LDS Blessing of children date. Dates for LDS Blessing of children should be recorded only in the notes. LDS baptism dates are recorded in the LDS ordinance fields.)

Additional marriages are recorded on the back of the form, and sealings of those marriages can follow the marriage detail. Some forms have space to indicate whether or not there is an additional marriage listed on the back of the form.

A list of abbreviations of LDS temples can be found in many places. Ask your ward or branch family history consultant where you may find one. The Personal Ancestral File genealogy software program lists them, as does the instruction booklet, *Come unto Christ Through Temple Ordinances and Covenants.*

Dates of ordinances previously performed can often be found in your own home or in the homes of relatives. These dates can also be found in the files of the LDS Church. An index to official temple ordinance records is available, known as the Ordinance Index. This is not yet a complete index to all temple ordinances performed. But the 1997 release contains most of the records for deceased persons for whom ordinances have been performed. There will always be records for persons who were members of the LDS Church who are now deceased but who were born within the last 110 years or married within the last 95 years whose records fit within the privacy guidelines and are not included because they are assumed living. In addition the proxy work done since the last edition was prepared for publication will not yet be included in the index.

You can use this on computer as part of FamilySearch at your local Family History Center or ward or stake meetinghouse. It is found on the FamilySearch menu under LDS Options. The Ordinance Index is presently composed of two parts: one created in 1993, called the Main Index, and an Addendum which is updated periodically. The most current one (in May 1998) was created and released in 1997.

There is a partial Ordinance Index (IGI) available on microfiche that goes only to 1992. It contains approximately 187 million records; while the 1993 index contains 200 million records, and the Addendum contains 84 million records; the complete 1997 release including the Main Ordinance Index and the Addendum contains 284 million records. Thus the microfiche edition is lacking 97 million records that are included in the FamilySearch edition of either the Ordinance Index or the International Genealogical Index (IGI).

Please note: Prior to the 1997 release of the Ordinance Index, the International Genealogical Index (IGI) was used both for research and for LDS ordinance checking. Beginning with the 1997 release, the two are separate. The IGI no longer contains LDS ordinance details, but it does contain the same records. The IGI is a marvelous research tool, which everyone should use in genealogical research. (See page 44.) Remember to keep a record of the names and ordinances you submit, because if you submit them again within a year or so, they will be cleared for duplicate ordinances. It is important for the family to keep their own records and to coordinate with relatives who may be working on the same lines.

C. Pedigree charts

Many pedigree charts include spaces to indicate the status of ordinances done. You can indicate with an X or by filling in the space that the ordinance is completed.

B=Baptism, E=Endowment; S=Sealing to spouse, P=Sealing to parents, and F=Family group, with all ordinances done for the children.

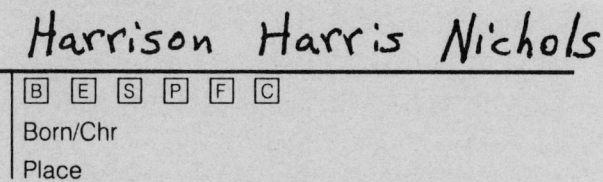

FIGURE 19 - LDS pedigree chart ordinance boxes

There is also an ordinance pedigree chart that shows 8 generations of your family, with limited information (names and space enough to add the years of birth and death, if desired), and the boxes for the ordinance status of each. One pedigree chart has four parts, each one beginning with a different grandparent and showing eight generations of his or her ancestors. It is available from the LDS Church distribution center near you or from your local Family History Center. Its item number is 31829.

The ordinance pedigree chart is an excellent way to get an overview of your family and to identify ordinances that may not yet be done or determine where research has not yet identified your ancestors.

It can also be used by people who are not members of the LDS Church to see an overview of their pedigree lines.

D. Names for temple ordinances

If you wish to submit names for LDS temple ordinances, first identify the persons and organize them into families. You can do this by filling out family group records and pedigree charts or by typing the information into a computer (see pages 7, 50).

After you have identified the persons, you need to determine whether the ordinances have already been performed for them. Because the Church has done millions of names taken from vital events of births, christenings, and marriages, the ordinances may already have been done even though you do not know of any family member who may have requested that it be done. Many also received these ordinances for themselves during their lifetimes. You can personally check the Ordinance Index and recognize many family members who may be listed there that others would not recognize because of the slight difference in the way the name, date, or place may be listed. (No outsider, including a computer, knows your family like you do.)

When you have the names identified and organized into families, they must be typed into a computer. You can type them into a home computer program (such as Personal Ancestral File®, see page 74), then take a diskette containing the information to the local Family History Center where the TempleReady™ program is part of the FamilySearch computer programs and files. Or you can type it directly into the TempleReady program at the meetinghouse. Either way, organize the information into families before you submit the names. (It is possible to submit a single name without knowing his or her family, but this is not the recommended way. And since the names we submit will be our own relatives, we can know at least some of the family members.)

- Whether you type the information into a genealogy software program first or directly into TempleReady has some definite advantages that you will want to be aware of.

1. If you have a computer (or can go to a relative or friend who has one) you can often do it at home, where you have all of your records and where you can do it when it is convenient to you.

2. When you type the information into PAF, you can use copies of the same information for many purposes; for example, to send to the temple using TempleReady, to send to Ancestral File, to send to cousin Robert and to Grandpa Nichols, and to keep for your own use.

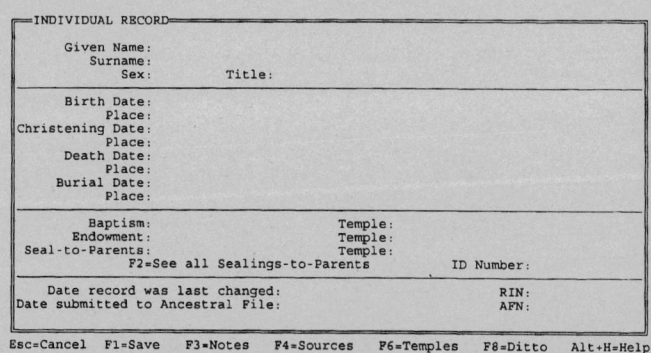

FIGURE 20 - *PAF 3.0 data entry screen showing LDS ordinances*

When you type the information into TempleReady, you cannot use it for any other purpose without retyping the information. (This is true as of May 1998. Anything to do with computer programs may change with a new release, so watch for possible upgrades and changes.)

3. You can be typing your information into PAF while someone else is using TempleReady to process names for temple work.

4. Even if you do not have a computer, and you must use the one at the meetinghouse or at the home of a friend, PAF requires less computer capacity and will be available on computers that do not have FamilySearch at the Church, or perhaps at the home of a friend.

5. The temple submission process in PAF will place "SUBMITTED" in the ordinance fields for each name where an ordinance was approved, thus helping you maintain your records of work submitted and avoid submitting the same names again.

Note: It is possible to use the regular GEDCOM rather than the Temple Submission GEDCOM, and there may be very rare circumstances when this is better. But this will not place the SUBMITTED notation in the LDS ordinance fields, and should not ordinarily be used.

If you do not have all of the information or relatives included in the GEDCOM file, when you get the names loaded into the TempleReady program you can add them by typing them. Be sure that you have printed copies of your family group records with you at the TempleReady site.

6. The temple submission process in PAF will look for duplicate records within that submission again helping you avoid submitting the same name twice for the same ordinance.

On the other hand:

7. The screen on the TempleReady program is easy to use.

8. You can type in only what you want to submit.

However, you should type in as much information as you know about the persons who are to receive ordinances, including their death detail, the names and birth date and place and death date for parents and spouse. These details are kept in the children's records or spouse's record, if the information is provided (though it does not show in the TempleReady report). It can then be available for future editions of the International Genealogical Index (IGI) and the Ordinance Index, when the format will display additional details. This will help avoid duplication later, as well as allow you to recognize the records of your own ancestors.

Caution: You must also be sure that you tell the system you do not want these names cleared for ordinances. (See figure 21.)

9. TempleReady will take names with less information when you cannot find the details of births and marriages. However, you can type these into the TempleReady program after uploading the rest of your PAF temple preparation file, which is recommended.

If you use the regular GEDCOM function to create a file to take to TempleReady where the names can be cleared for temple ordinances, you will need to type in SUBMITTED for each of the appropriate ordinances and do your own checking to see that there is no duplication of the same name within your submission. (The PAF program does these tasks for you in the temple preparation process.)

E. Duplicate checking (for ordinances already done)

Important Note: While TempleReady will do an automatic check of selected records from the Ordinance Index (including the Main section and the Addendum) as part of the processing of the names for temple work, it will not always identify the duplicate entries in the file; in addition, the Ordinance Index does not contain records of all ordinances performed. You need to help in the effort to avoid duplicating ordinances already done.

Ways you may help:

- Use your own personal knowledge.

    If you know that someone has been through the temple and had their ordinances performed, do not submit the name. You do not need the date that the ordinance was done. You can record "No" in TempleReady to the question "Do you wish to have the ordinances done?" or record "completed" in your PAF file, or write DONE or PS (previously submitted) or anything else you wish in your own records. TempleReady will not allow you to type in an ordinance date, so do not waste your time finding the exact date for this purpose.

- Use records in your own home, or in the homes of relatives.

    Some of the ordinances done before 1970, those recently done, and those for persons born within the past 95 years are not yet in the Ordinance Index, yet they are often in family records. Take the time to look in these records to determine which ordinances have been done.

- Check Ancestral File. Many of the ordinance dates that are not yet in the Ordinance Index or for whom you do not recognize them in the Ordinance Index context but where you will recognize them in the family group setting are in Ancestral File.

  Particularly if your family were members of the LDS Church while living, or if you have had relatives who were doing temple work or research work and submitting names, or if your ancestry goes back to New England or to countries from which early Church members came, check Ancestral File before submitting the names for temple ordinances.

- Check the Ordinance Index personally.

  The computer helps and can do many things better than we can, but other things we can do better. When it comes to recognizing your own relatives, even when the information is slightly different in the file, you can do much better than the computer. If you have the computer display the names where your ancestor would be listed, you can quickly browse the file and recognize records of your relatives that the computer cannot recognize. Check the Ordinance Index yourself, especially for direct ancestors and their families.

For example, when the Ordinance Index lists an Isaac Hoyt born in Connecticut and your record lists him as born in New York (and you know the two places overlap), TempleReady will not even consider the possibility that the Connecticut record could be the same as the New York record, because the state is different. But you can see this with your eyes and your knowledge of the area. TempleReady uses a very limited locality area to search, such as exact counties in British areas and Scandinavia (Denmark, Sweden, Norway), providences in Canada, and states in Germany and the USA.

Note: While it is anticipated that future editions of the Ordinance Index will contain more information on many of the names recorded there (such as death dates), as well as many more names, the present edition is very limited in the amount of detail as well as incomplete in containing total names that have had ordinances done. The LDS Church encourages its members to do what they reasonably can to determine if the ordinances have already been done and to pray about which names to submit.

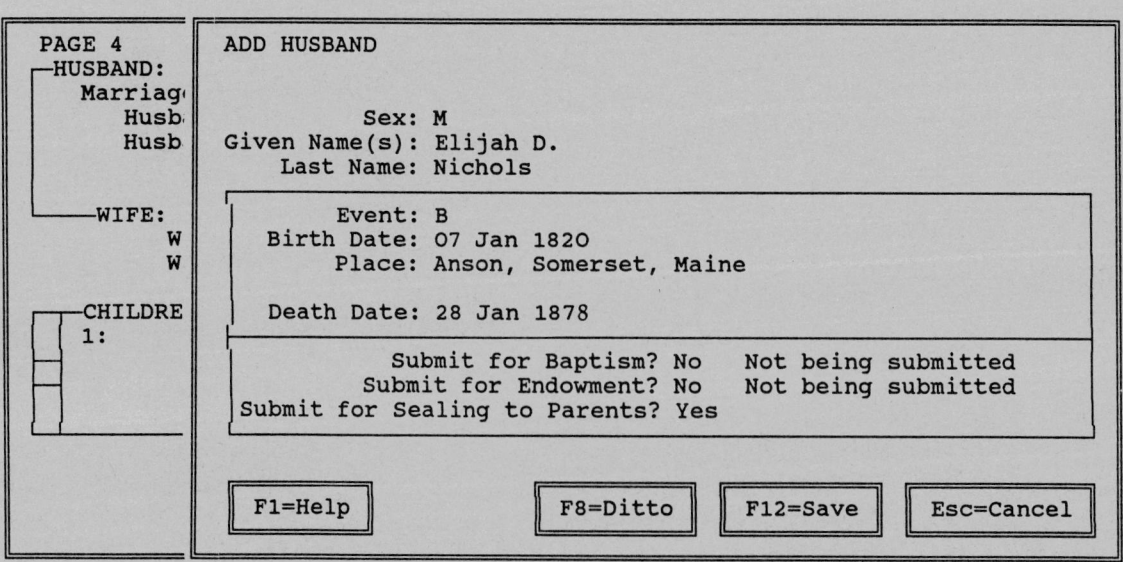

FIGURE 21 - *You can answer these questions in TempleReady*

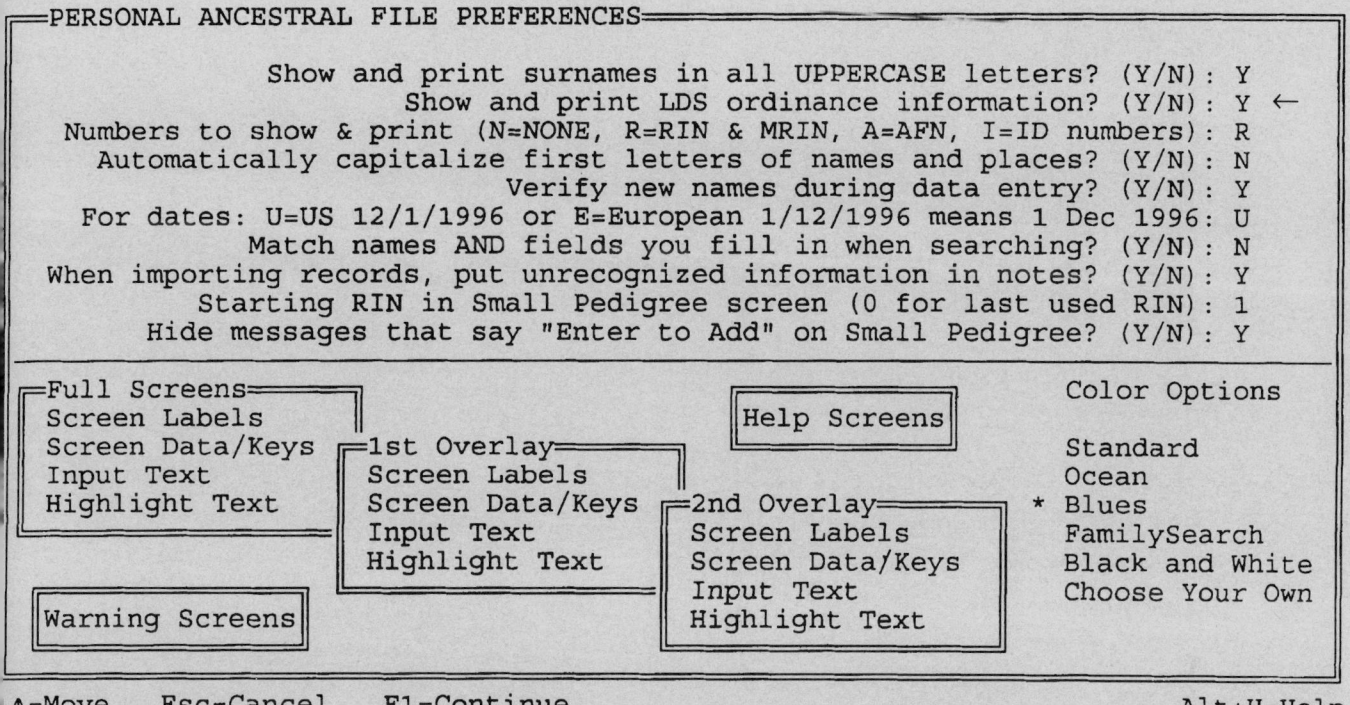

FIGURE 22 - PAF Preferences screen

Computer software programs to record LDS ordinances

- Many software programs have the ability to create fields for you to use for whatever labels or tags you want. Others provide specifically for LDS ordinance fields. The Personal Ancestral File (PAF) provides these fields for you. (For more information about PAF, see Glossary and page 50.)

To display LDS ordinance fields on the PAF screens (to allow you to enter them, and to see them in screen displays, and to print them out), answer Y for YES on the line that states

Show and print LDS ordinance information

This appears in the Utility menu, where you select Preferences. (See figure 22.)

You can have a default to show these ordinance dates and still change information that prints by your selections in the print menu choices. Both Ancestral File and the Ordinance Index display LDS ordinance dates. (The IGI does not, beginning with the 1997 release.)

You can download records including these dates, or without ordinance dates, from these FamilySearch files. See page 44 for more information on FamilySearch. See the separate publications, *Genealogy in the Computer Age: Understanding FamilySearch®*, volumes 1 and 2 (Salt Lake City: Family History Educators), for detailed descriptions and illustrations of FamilySearch resource files.

VIII. ADDING TO YOUR FOUNDATION (MORE THAN NAMES)

A. Photographs

It is fascinating to see what our ancestors and other relatives looked like. We may see "Cousin Watson's nose" or "Cousin Grant's chin" in the picture of Grandpa Harrison Nichols, for example, or in Dad when he was a child.

Let others know that you are interested in copies of pictures. They may have extra copies or may be willing to have copies made for you. Remember that it takes money to have copies made, so don't ask unless you are in a position to volunteer to pay

FIGURE 23 - *Photos can be fun*

the expenses. (Sometimes, however, older relatives are only too glad to find someone who will cherish their treasured pictures after they are gone.)

A portrait pedigree chart is a fun thing to compile. This brings together pictures of your direct ancestors.

Be sure to identify all pictures that you have. There are few things more frustrating than to have treasured old pictures but not to know who they are or when the pictures were taken.

Check with your library for instruction books that will tell you about care of old pictures.

Advancing technology. As computer technology has advanced, the ability to share and use photographs has been greatly enhanced. It is now quite easy to incorporate them into your family history projects.

First, scan your pictures. This can be done with a regular scanner, or with more simple software that just scans photographs. This process takes a picture of the photograph or snapshot and stores it in digital form within the computer. These pictures can be stored on a diskette, on the hard drive, or now on a compact disc. They do take a fairly large amount of storage space. A Zip drive, which stores compressed files of your computer data, may be a good thing to have. If you do not have the scanner, you can often find someone who does and with whom you can work out an agreement to have them scan selected pictures for you, or take them to a local photocopy store that provides this service.

Once scanned, you can then use the pictures in most word processing programs, and in some genealogy computer programs. Import the scanned picture through graphics, as an image. (Some word processors will accept images with most endings or extensions, such as .tif, while others will not. For example, WordPerfect 6.1 will take a .tif ending, but not some others; its version 8.0 will take more graphics extensions.) Within a word processor, you can add captions, borders (frames), change the size of the picture to suit your needs, etc. The menu will appear as part of the Graphics features, or you can often right-click your mouse on the inside of the picture and the menu will appear on your screen.

There are add-on programs that can help you produce a book from your genealogy software, such as Personal Ancestral File. For example, one such program is called the Personal Ancestral File Companion. This is available from the same publisher as PAF for only $10. It is a Windows program that allows you to use the Windows printer drivers to produce better quality printouts of pedigree charts, family groups, and other reports. The PAF Companion also allows you to transfer information, including genealogical detail, notes, and sources (if you want all of these, and LDS ordinance detail if you choose to include it) into your word processor, such as WordPerfect. The preliminary work is all done. You can then add scanned pictures if you wish and place them anywhere in the text. When you have it to suit you (adding more text, such as biographical detail if you wish), press a key and generate an index. The information will be arranged in paragraph form. Then you can simply print your very own book.

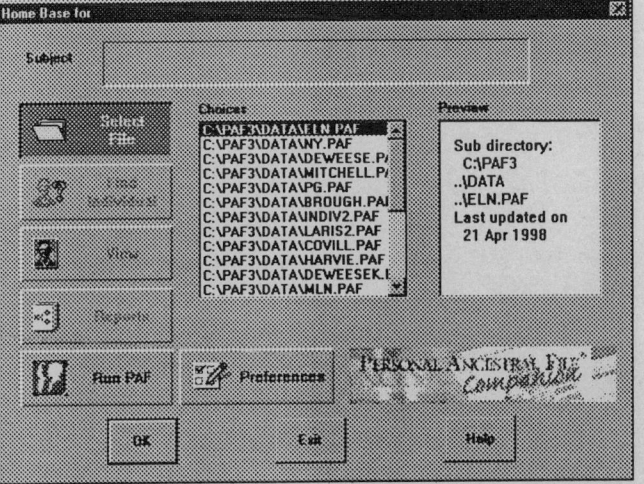

FIGURE 23A - *Personal Ancestral File® Companion: select the PAF 3.0 file from which you wish to print reports*

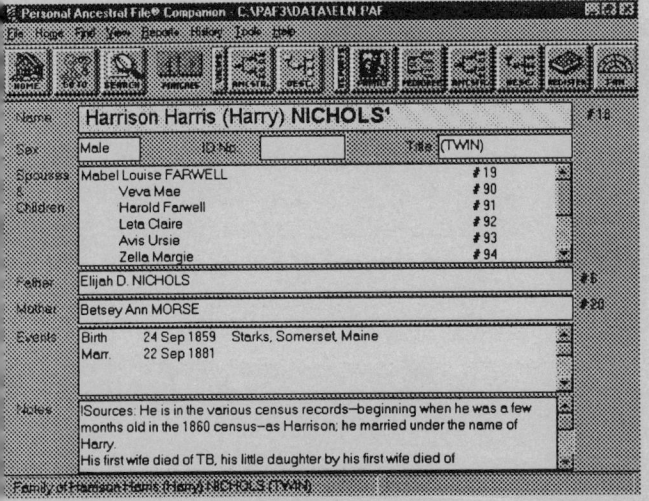

FIGURE 23B - *Personal Ancestral File® Companion: select the type of report from the choices at the top of the screen*

Another such program is called GEN-BOOK, available for $59 from 2105 Country Lane, Auburn CA 95603-9735, phone 916-889-9735; e-mail genbook@foothill.net (current 1998). It allows you to create a book of either descendants or ancestors and their families. All you need to do is press a few keys, and it will take your data from the PAF data file and generate a book into your word processor, such as WordPerfect. There are various options that you choose or you can accept the defaults. For example, you can include or exclude notes or sources; you can have the sources print in small print as footnotes; you can have the index in three columns (which saves a lot of paper) or two columns; you can include or exclude LDS ordinance detail. After you have generated the book into your word processor, you can then import your scanned images (pictures) and place them where you want them. You can also add any additional biographical or historical details that you wish. Then create an index in the usual manner in your word processor (in WordPerfect, this takes just a couple of key strokes). Then print it out. It will be in paragraph format. It makes a very nice book. There is a version to use with PAF, and another version of GEN-BOOK to use with any GEDCOM file.

Note: If you do not get clear pictures printed from GEN-BOOK, it is possible that you need to make some adjustments in your word processor and printer preferences. If you can print clear pictures from your word processor using other programs, make sure the document setting of print quality within the print selection of your word processor is on high (not medium); and the same in your printer preferences.

If you do not get clear pictures printed from your regular word processing documents, it may be the printer. A printer may print words well, but not graphics. Check the number of dpi (dots per inch). A printer with 600 dpi usually prints pictures well. You may need to take your document someplace where they have a printer that will handle graphics.

Several of the genealogy programs, such as Roots or Family Tree Maker™, allow scanned images (pictures) to be imported directly into their programs without transferring the data to a word processor. This has advantages and disadvantages. Check your software instructions for details of what your program will do.

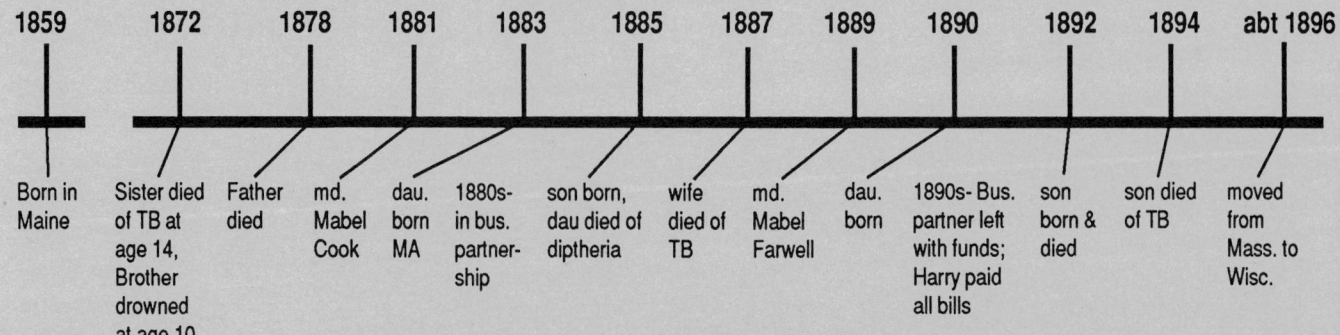

FIGURE 24 - A time line

A new option for storage of your scanned pictures is on a CD ROM disc. There is software now available that will allow you to both read and to write to compact discs. This provides an excellent means of preserving your treasured pictures, as well as a good way to share them. You may also be able to find pictures in books or on-line databases that are of interest to you that can be added to your collection. Software may allow you to just read, or just write, or both, on a compact disc.

B. Time lines

You may enjoy showing the events of a person's life in graphic form. Draw a straight horizontal line, which represent one's life. Then draw vertical lines to show events. If there are only three months between events, the space shown is smaller than if there are ten years between events. It can be on any scale you wish both as to the size of the paper and the amount of detail. Using brown butcher paper, you can have an unlimited time line. It should contain at least ten events. It can be used to show migrations (moves), job changes, growing-up years, and more. (See figure 24.)

C. Family heritage

Another exciting and fascinating facet of genealogy and family history can be called family heritage. Genealogical facts represent people who experienced life, as we do. What were their joys, fears, achievements, disappointments, and goals? What was their philosophy of life? What did they do for a living? How did they feel about it? What were their feelings about their country, their religion, their neighbors, their needs, their desires? What types of things made them happy or sad or afraid or courageous? How were these feelings expressed in their actions, attitudes, and lives?

The answers to these and many related questions are found through a study of family heritage, and may have been or are yet to be recorded as family history

The foundation of family heritage is genealogy. You must first know who these people were and when and where they lived, as well as who their other family members were.

But family heritage goes beyond genealogical facts. Look for it in your own heart and mind and in what you have been taught is important. Look for it in the oral history, traditions, and philosophies that have been passed down to you. Look for it in the keepsakes, heirlooms, and treasured things within your own family. Look for it in the heritage of thoughts and feelings and traditions that have been passed to you.

As you study this kind of family history, you will find that history has not changed as much as we are often led to believe. People are still people, and the fears, joys, happiness, worries, and the things that made life meaningful to our ancestors are still the things that make life meaningful to us today. It doesn't matter whether our way of living is different, or if our methods of preparing a meal or doing the laundry is different, or the way we get from one place to another has changed. It is still the feelings of the heart that make for happiness or misery; the feeling that a person is contributing something to someone that provides a sense of self-worth and self-esteem; the feeling that there is a Supreme Being who watches over us and loves us — such feelings conquer fear and provide serenity of heart and soul to all people of all ages and times.

A study of family history increases one's understanding of the universal relationship of all people It strengthens ties with living family members and bridges generation gaps as we see again that the history of the human race is really the history of individual persons and families. We inherit what our ancestors have planned and worked and prayed for us to have. Generations yet unborn will inherit what we bequeath to them. What will it be? Now is the time when we decide what heritage we will pass on to them.

Family heritage is the story of families — yours and mine. We are not looking for kings and heroes, just to identify our own ancestors. As they must accept their descendants, so we must accept them. You will find many unsung heroes and heroines who simply went honestly and dutifully about their daily humble tasks and gave to us the honorable and wonderful heritage that we enjoy today.

For more information on family heritage, see the publication *Teaching Family Heritage in Four Weeks: A Course Outline* (Salt Lake City, Utah: Family History Educators, 1990). Although you may not be planning to teach others, it can give you excellent ideas for your own family heritage project.

Do your ancestors come from early United States pioneers, from England, Ireland, Scotland, Denmark, Germany, Taiwan, Africa, France? When did they leave their native land and why?

Action: Write down what you know or have heard about your national origins. Write down everything you know, then begin to ask questions.

Write down at least one incident from your own life or that of an ancestor, something you think would be interesting to others. It can be humorous, sad, tragic, or sacred. When you have time, add more incidents. You have just started recording your family history.

APPENDIX A

A list of a few nationally known genealogical societies and national research facilities with their addresses:

National Genealogical Society
4527 Seventeenth Street
North Arlington, VA 22207-2399

New England Historic Genealogical Society
101 Newbury Street
Boston, MA 02116

Family History Library of The Church of Jesus Christ of Latter-day Saints (LDS, Mormons)
35 West North Temple Street
Salt Lake City, UT 84150

(Genealogical Society of Utah is an affiliate of the LDS Church)

Family History Centers (branches of this library) can be found in many cities throughout the world. Look in telephone directories under the name of the Church or check the Internet at *www.lds.org*.

National Archives
Washington, DC 20025
Its field branches:

Atlanta
1557 St. Joseph Ave.
East Point, GA 30344

States Served: Alabama, Georgia, Florida, Kentucky, Mississippi, North Carolina, South Carolina, Tennessee

Boston
380 Trapelo Road
Waltham MA 02154

States served: Connecticut, Maine, Massachusetts, New Hampshire, Rhode Island, Vermont

Chicago
7358 South Pulaski Road
Chicago, IL 60629

States served: Illinois, Indiana, Michigan, Minnesota, Ohio, Wisconsin

Denver
Building 48, Denver Federal Center
Denver, CO 80225

States served: Colorado, Montana, North Dakota, South Dakota, Utah, Wyoming

Fort Worth
501 West Felix Street (location)
P.O. Box 6216 (mailing)
Fort Worth, TX 76115

States served: Arkansas, Louisiana, New Mexico, Oklahoma, Texas

Kansas City
2306 East Bannister Road
Kansas City, MO 64131

States served: Iowa, Kansas, Missouri, Nebraska

Los Angeles
24000 Avila Road
Laguna Niguel, CA 92677

States served: Arizona, southern California (counties of Imperial, Inyo, Kern, Los Angeles, Orange, Riverside, San Bernardino, San Diego, San Luis Obispo, Santa Barbara, Ventura), Nevada (Clark County only)

New York
Building 22 MOT Bayonne
Bayonne, NJ 07002

States served: New Jersey, New York, Puerto Rico, the Virgin Islands

Philadelphia
GSA Regional Office Building
Room 1350, 9th and Market Streets
Philadelphia, PA 19107

States served: Delaware, Pennsylvania, Maryland, Virginia, West Virginia

San Francisco
1000 Commodore Dr.
San Bruno, CA 94066

States served: Hawaii, Nevada (except Clark County), California (except counties shown for the Los Angeles branch), and American Samoa

Seattle
6125 Sand Point NE
Seattle, WA 98115

States served: Alaska, Idaho, Oregon, and Washington

Library of Congress
Washington, DC 20025

National Society Daughters of the American Revolution (DAR)
1776 D Street NW,
Washington, DC 20006-5392

Federation of Genealogical Societies (FGS)
Business office address changes with officer change; contact your local genealogical society or library and ask them for the current address of FGS.

Many local colleges and universities offer courses in family history or genealogy. Brigham Young University, Provo, Utah 84602 offers a home study course, as does the National Genealogical Society (address above).

APPENDIX B

Forms pedigree charts and family group records (Regular and LDS)

The following sample forms are:

FIGURE 25- Blank pedigree chart (page 33)

FIGURE 26- Blank pedigree chart with LDS ordinance status boxes (page 34)

FIGURE 27- Blank family group record form (page 35)

FIGURE 28- Blank family group record form with LDS ordinance fields (page 36)

FIGURE 29- Pedigree chart with information (page 37) (printed from the Personal Ancestral File® Companion)

FIGURE 30- Family group record with information (page 38) (printed from the Personal Ancestral File® Companion)

Ancestor Chart

Name of Compiler_____   Person No. 1 on this chart is the same person as No._____ on chart No._____.   Chart No._____

Address_____

City, State_____

Date_____

b. — Date of Birth
p.b. — Place of Birth
m. — Date of Marriage
d. — Date of Death
p.d. — Place of Death

2 _____ (Father of No. 1)
  b.
  p.b.
  m.
  d.
  p.d

4 _____ (Father of No. 2)
  b.
  p.b.
  m.
  d.
  p.d

5 _____ (Mother of No. 2)
  b.
  p.b.
  d.
  p.d.

8 _____ (Father of No. 4)
  b.
  p.b.
  m.
  d.
  p.d

9 _____ (Mother of No. 4)
  b.
  p.b.
  d.
  p.d

10 _____ (Father of No. 5)
  b.
  p.b.
  m.
  d.
  p.d

11 _____ (Mother of No. 5)
  b.
  p.b.
  d.
  p.d.

16 b. (Father of No. 8, Cont. on chart No._____)
   m.
   d.

17 b. (Mother of No. 8, Cont. on chart No._____)
   d.

18 b. (Father of No. 9, Cont. on chart No._____)
   m.
   d.

19 b. (Mother of No. 9, Cont. on chart No._____)
   d.

20 b. (Father of No. 10, Cont. on chart No._____)
   m.
   d.

21 b. (Mother of No. 10, Cont. on chart No._____)
   d.

22 b. (Father of No. 11, Cont. on chart No._____)
   m.
   d.

23 b. (Mother of No. 11, Cont. on chart No._____)
   d.

3 _____ (Mother of No. 1)
  b.
  p.b.
  d.
  p.d.

6 _____ (Father of No. 3)
  b.
  p.b.
  m.
  d.
  p.d

7 _____ (Mother of No. 3)
  b.
  p.b.
  d.
  p.d.

12 _____ (Father of No. 6)
  b.
  p.b.
  m.
  d.
  p.d

13 _____ (Mother of No. 6)
  b.
  p.b.
  d.
  p.d.

14 _____ (Father of No. 7)
  b.
  p.b.
  m.
  d.
  p.d

15 _____ (Mother of No. 7)
  b.
  p.b.
  d.
  p.d.

24 b. (Father of No. 12, Cont. on chart No._____)
   m.
   d.

25 b. (Mother of No. 12, Cont. on chart No._____)
   d.

26 b. (Father of No. 13, Cont. on chart No._____)
   m.
   d.

27 b. (Mother of No. 13, Cont. on chart No._____)
   d.

28 b. (Father of No. 14, Cont. on chart No._____)
   m.
   d.

29 b. (Mother of No. 14, Cont. on chart No._____)
   d.

30 b. (Father of No. 15, Cont. on chart No._____)
   m.
   d.

31 b. (Mother of No. 15, Cont. on chart No._____)
   d.

_____ (Spouse of No. 1)

Pedigree Chart

Chart no. _____

No. 1 on this chart is the same as No. _____ on chart no. _____.

Mark boxes when ordinances are completed.
- [B] Baptized
- [E] Endowed
- [SP] Sealed to parents
- [SS] Sealed to spouse
- [F] Family Group Record exists for this couple
- [C] Children's ordinances completed

2 (Father) [B] [E] [SP] [SS] [F] [C]
When born
Where
When married
Where
When died
Where

4 (Father of no. 2) [B] [E] [SP] [SS] [F] [C]
When born
Where
When married
Where
When died
Where

8 (Father of no. 4) [B] [E] [SP] [SS] [F] [C] Cont. on chart n____
When born
Where
When married
When died
Where

9 (Mother of no. 4) [B] [E] [SP] [SS] Cont. chart n____
When born
Where
When died
Where

5 (Mother of no. 2) [B] [E] [SP] [SS]
When born
Where
When died
Where

10 (Father of no. 5) [B] [E] [SP] [SS] [F] [C] Cont. on chart n____
When born
Where
When married
When died
Where

11 (Mother of no. 5) [B] [E] [SP] [SS] Cont. chart n____
When born
Where
When died
Where

1 _____
(Name) [B] [E] [SP] [SS] [F] [C]
When born
Where
When married
Where
When died
Where

_____
(Spouse) [B] [E] [SP] [SS]

3 ((Mother) [B] [E] [SP] [SS]
When born
Where
When died
Where

6 (Father of no. 3) [B] [E] [SP] [SS] [F] [C]
When born
Where
When married
Where
When died
Where

12 (Father of no. 6) [B] [E] [SP] [SS] [F] [C] Cont. chart n____
When born
Where
When married
When died
Where

13 (Mother of no. 6) [B] [E] [SP] [SS] Cont. chart n____
When born
Where
When died
Where

7 (Mother of no. 3) [B] [E] [SP] [SS]
When born
Where
When died
Where

14 (Father of no. 7) [B] [E] [SP] [SS] [F] [C] Cont. chart ____
When born
Where
When married
When died
Where

15 (Mother of no. 7) [B] [E] [SP] [SS] Cont. chart ____
When born
Where
When died
Where

Your name and address

Telephone number | Date prepared

Published by The Church of Jesus Christ of Latter-day Saints   2/96   Printed in USA   31826

FAMILY GROUP NO. _____

Husband's Full Name _____

This information Obtained From:

Husband's Data	Day Month Year	City, Town or Place	County or Province, etc.	State or Country	Add. Info. on Husband
Birth					
Chr'nd					
Marr.					
Death					
Burial					

Places of Residence

Occupation — Church Affiliation — Military Rec.

Other wives, if any. No. (1) (2) etc.
Make separate sheet for each marr.

His Father _____ Mother's Maiden Name _____

Wife's Full Maiden Name

Wife's Data	Day Month Year	City, Town or Place	County or Province, etc.	State or Country	Add. Info. on Wife
Birth					
Chr'nd					
Death					
Burial					

Compiler _____

Address _____

City, State _____

Date _____

Places of Residence

Occupation — Church Affiliation — Military Rec.

Other husbands, if any. No. (1) (2) etc.
Make separate sheet for each marr.

Her Father _____ Mother's Maiden Name _____

Sex	Children's Names in Full (Arrange in order of birth)	Children's Data	Day Month Year	City, Town or Place	County or Province, etc.	State or Country	Add. info. on Children
	1	Birth					
		Marr.					
	Full Name of Spouse	Death					
		Burial					
	2	Birth					
		Marr.					
	Full Name of Spouse	Death					
		Burial					
	3	Birth					
		Marr.					
	Full Name of Spouse	Death					
		Burial					
	4	Birth					
		Marr.					
	Full Name of Spouse	Death					
		Burial					
	5	Birth					
		Marr.					
	Full Name of Spouse	Death					
		Burial					
	6	Birth					
		Marr.					
	Full Name of Spouse	Death					
		Burial					
	7	Birth					
		Marr.					
	Full Name of Spouse	Death					
		Burial					
	8	Birth					
		Marr.					
	Full Name of Spouse	Death					
		Burial					
	9	Birth					
		Marr.					
	Full Name of Spouse	Death					
		Burial					
	10	Birth					
		Marr.					
	Full Name of Spouse	Death					
		Burial					

*For additional children use Everton Publishers' Children Continuation Sheet, Form A11

Family Group Record

If typing, set spacing at 1 1/2.   Page ___ of ___

Write date as: 4 Oct. 1896

Husband Given name(s)		Last name		☐ See " marri
Born (day month year)	Place		LDS ordinance dates	Temp
Christened	Place		Baptized	
Died	Place		Endowed	
Buried	Place		Sealed to parents	
Married	Place		Sealed to spouse	
Husband's father Given name(s)		Last name		☐ Dece
Husband's mother Given name(s)		Maiden name		☐ Dece

Wife Given name(s)		Maiden name		☐ See " marri
Born (day month year)	Place		LDS ordinance dates	Temp
Christened	Place		Baptized	
Died	Place		Endowed	
Buried	Place		Sealed to parents	
Wife's father Given name(s)		Last name		☐ Dece
Wife's mother Given name(s)		Maiden name		☐ Dece

Children List each child (whether living or dead) in order of birth.   LDS ordinance dates   Temp

1 Sex | Given name(s) | Last name | ☐ See ' marri

Born (day month year)	Place	Baptized
Christened	Place	Endowed
Died	Place	Sealed to parents
Spouse Given name(s)		Last name
Married	Place	Sealed to spouse

2 Sex | Given name(s) | Last name | ☐ See ' marri

Born (day month year)	Place	Baptized
Christened	Place	Endowed
Died	Place	Sealed to parents
Spouse Given name(s)		Last name
Married	Place	Sealed to spouse

3 Sex | Given name(s) | Last name | ☐ See marri

Born (day month year)	Place	Baptized
Christened	Place	Endowed
Died	Place	Sealed to parents
Spouse Given name(s)		Last name
Married	Place	Sealed to spouse

Write place as: Tryon, Polk, North Carolina, USA or St. Martins, Birmingham, Warwick, Eng.

Select **only one** of the following options. The option you select applies to all names on this form.

☐ **Option 1—Family File** Send all names to my family file at the _____ Temple.

☐ **Option 2—Temple File** Send all names to any temple, and assign proxies for all approved ordinances.

☐ **Option 3—Ancestral File™** Send all names to the computerized Ancestral File for research purposes only, not for ordinances. I am including the required pedigree chart.

Your name

Address

Phone ( )

Date prepared

Published by The Church of Jesus Christ of Latter-day Saints 10/93 Printed in USA

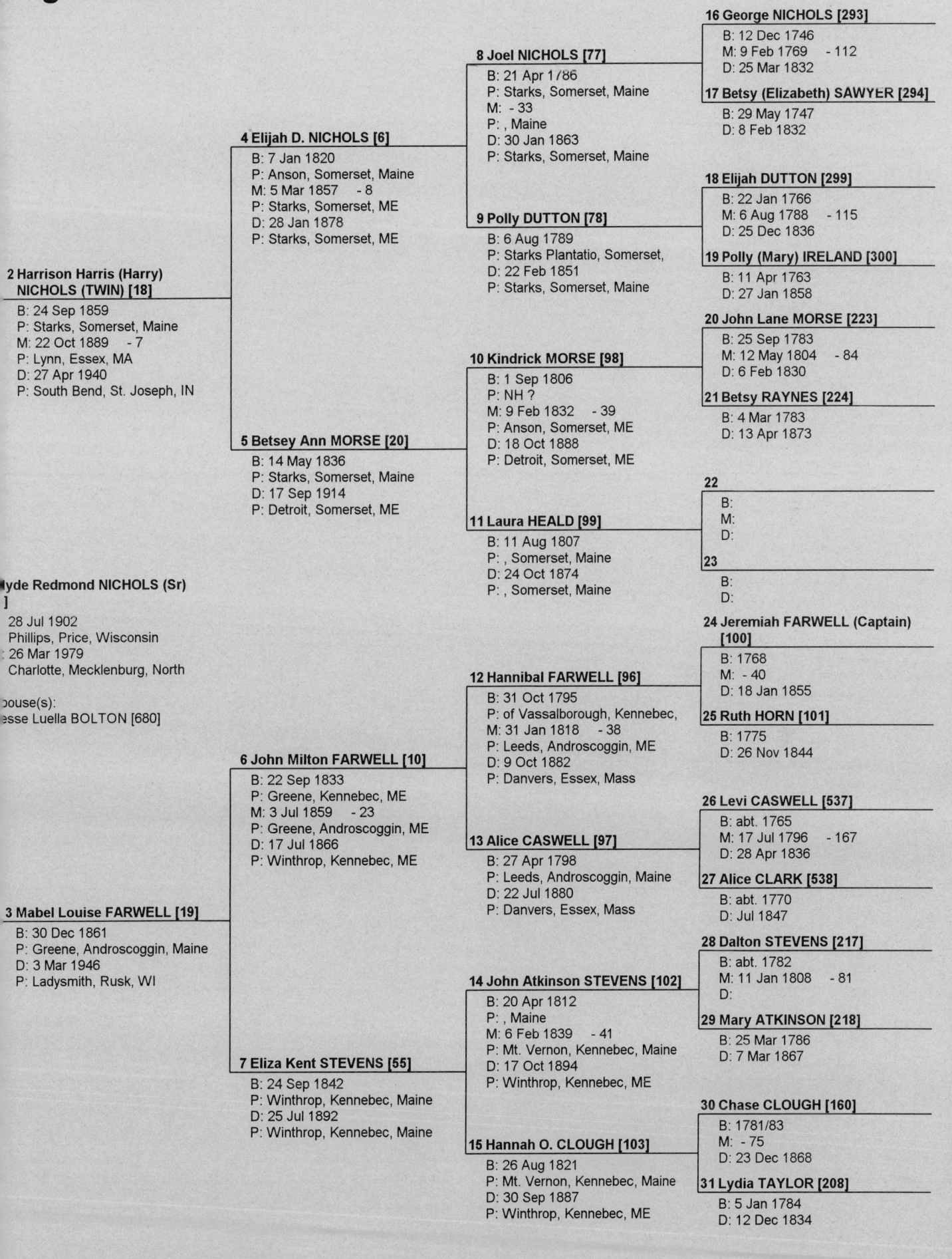

Pedigree Chart

Chart no. 1

2 Harrison Harris (Harry) NICHOLS (TWIN) [18]
B: 24 Sep 1859
P: Starks, Somerset, Maine
M: 22 Oct 1889   - 7
P: Lynn, Essex, MA
D: 27 Apr 1940
P: South Bend, St. Joseph, IN

4 Elijah D. NICHOLS [6]
B: 7 Jan 1820
P: Anson, Somerset, Maine
M: 5 Mar 1857   - 8
P: Starks, Somerset, ME
D: 28 Jan 1878
P: Starks, Somerset, ME

5 Betsey Ann MORSE [20]
B: 14 May 1836
P: Starks, Somerset, Maine
D: 17 Sep 1914
P: Detroit, Somerset, ME

8 Joel NICHOLS [77]
B: 21 Apr 1786
P: Starks, Somerset, Maine
M: - 33
P: , Maine
D: 30 Jan 1863
P: Starks, Somerset, Maine

9 Polly DUTTON [78]
B: 6 Aug 1789
P: Starks Plantatio, Somerset,
D: 22 Feb 1851
P: Starks, Somerset, Maine

10 Kindrick MORSE [98]
B: 1 Sep 1806
P: NH ?
M: 9 Feb 1832   - 39
P: Anson, Somerset, ME
D: 18 Oct 1888
P: Detroit, Somerset, ME

11 Laura HEALD [99]
B: 11 Aug 1807
P: , Somerset, Maine
D: 24 Oct 1874
P: , Somerset, Maine

16 George NICHOLS [293]
B: 12 Dec 1746
M: 9 Feb 1769   - 112
D: 25 Mar 1832

17 Betsy (Elizabeth) SAWYER [294]
B: 29 May 1747
D: 8 Feb 1832

18 Elijah DUTTON [299]
B: 22 Jan 1766
M: 6 Aug 1788   - 115
D: 25 Dec 1836

19 Polly (Mary) IRELAND [300]
B: 11 Apr 1763
D: 27 Jan 1858

20 John Lane MORSE [223]
B: 25 Sep 1783
M: 12 May 1804   - 84
D: 6 Feb 1830

21 Betsy RAYNES [224]
B: 4 Mar 1783
D: 13 Apr 1873

22
B:
M:
D:

23
B:
D:

---

lyde Redmond NICHOLS (Sr)
28 Jul 1902
Phillips, Price, Wisconsin
26 Mar 1979
Charlotte, Mecklenburg, North
ouse(s):
esse Luella BOLTON [680]

3 Mabel Louise FARWELL [19]
B: 30 Dec 1861
P: Greene, Androscoggin, Maine
D: 3 Mar 1946
P: Ladysmith, Rusk, WI

6 John Milton FARWELL [10]
B: 22 Sep 1833
P: Greene, Kennebec, ME
M: 3 Jul 1859   - 23
P: Greene, Androscoggin, ME
D: 17 Jul 1866
P: Winthrop, Kennebec, ME

7 Eliza Kent STEVENS [55]
B: 24 Sep 1842
P: Winthrop, Kennebec, Maine
D: 25 Jul 1892
P: Winthrop, Kennebec, Maine

12 Hannibal FARWELL [96]
B: 31 Oct 1795
P: of Vassalborough, Kennebec,
M: 31 Jan 1818   - 38
P: Leeds, Androscoggin, ME
D: 9 Oct 1882
P: Danvers, Essex, Mass

13 Alice CASWELL [97]
B: 27 Apr 1798
P: Leeds, Androscoggin, Maine
D: 22 Jul 1880
P: Danvers, Essex, Mass

14 John Atkinson STEVENS [102]
B: 20 Apr 1812
P: , Maine
M: 6 Feb 1839   - 41
P: Mt. Vernon, Kennebec, Maine
D: 17 Oct 1894
P: Winthrop, Kennebec, ME

15 Hannah O. CLOUGH [103]
B: 26 Aug 1821
P: Mt. Vernon, Kennebec, Maine
D: 30 Sep 1887
P: Winthrop, Kennebec, ME

24 Jeremiah FARWELL (Captain) [100]
B: 1768
M: - 40
D: 18 Jan 1855

25 Ruth HORN [101]
B: 1775
D: 26 Nov 1844

26 Levi CASWELL [537]
B: abt. 1765
M: 17 Jul 1796   - 167
D: 28 Apr 1836

27 Alice CLARK [538]
B: abt. 1770
D: Jul 1847

28 Dalton STEVENS [217]
B: abt. 1782
M: 11 Jan 1808   - 81
D:

29 Mary ATKINSON [218]
B: 25 Mar 1786
D: 7 Mar 1867

30 Chase CLOUGH [160]
B: 1781/83
M: - 75
D: 23 Dec 1868

31 Lydia TAYLOR [208]
B: 5 Jan 1784
D: 12 Dec 1834

Family Group Record

Harrison Harris (Harry) NICHOLS (TWIN) / Mabel Louise FARWELL MRIN 7
C:\PAF3\DATA\ELN.PAF
24 Jun 1998

Husband's Name: Harrison Harris (Harry) NICHOLS (TWIN) — RIN 18

Born	24 Sep 1859	Place	Starks, Somerset, Maine
Chr.			
Mar.	22 Oct 1889	Place	Lynn, Essex, MA
Died	27 Apr 1940	Place	South Bend, St. Joseph, IN
Bur.		Place	Ladysmith, Rusk, WI

Father: Elijah D. NICHOLS — RIN 6
Mother: Betsey Ann MORSE — RIN 20
Parent Link
Husband's other wives: Mabel COOK — RIN 1305
Parents' MRIN 8

Wife's Name: Mabel Louise FARWELL — RIN 19

Born	30 Dec 1861	Place	Greene, Androscoggin, Maine
Chr.			
Died	3 Mar 1946	Place	Ladysmith, Rusk, WI
Bur.			

Father: John Milton FARWELL — RIN 10
Mother: Eliza Kent STEVENS — RIN 55
Parent Link
Wife's other husbands:
Parents' MRIN 23

Children

1. Veva Mae NICHOLS — F — RIN 90

Born	29 Oct 1890	Place	Lynn, Essex, Mass
Chr.			
Mar.	24 Jun 1926	Place	
Died	12 May 1961	Place	, Michigan
Bur.			

Spouse: William Arthur CRAMER — RIN 171 — MRIN 62

2. Harold Farwell NICHOLS — M — RIN 91

Born	24 May 1892	Place	Lynn, Essex, Mass
Chr.			
Mar.			
Died	25 May 1892	Place	Lynn, Essex, Mass
Bur.			

Spouse:

3. Leta Claire NICHOLS — F — RIN 92

Born	11 May 1893	Place	Lynn, Essex, Mass
Chr.			
Mar.	3 Jul 1916	Place	Ladysmith, Rusk, Wisconsin
Died	11 Dec 1983	Place	Ladysmith, Rusk, Wisc
Bur.			

Spouse: Edward Clifton WOODBURY — RIN 172 — MRIN 63

4. Avis Ursie NICHOLS — F — RIN 93

Born	15 Mar 1895	Place	Cliftondale, Essex, Mass
Chr.			
Mar.	20 Jun 1945	Place	Ladysmith, Rusk, Wisc
Died			
Bur.			

Spouse: Orville Charles SMITH — RIN 173 — MRIN 64

[X] Check here if other children are listed on additional pages.

PART TWO: COMPUTERS AND FAMILY HISTORY/GENEALOGY

FIGURE 31 - A computer

I. LEARNING ABOUT COMPUTERS

A. If you've never used a computer

You do not have to know all the details of computers to be able to use them. Just as you can enjoy the use of electricity by simply knowing how to turn on a light switch, you can use computers after learning only a few basic details.

A computer keyboard is much like a typewriter. You will enjoy your computer work more if you know the finger positions taught in typewriting classes. You can also use the common "hunt and peck" system effectively.

The computer keyboard has more keys than a typewriter has. Of special importance to you are the keys with both letters and numbers on the same key. These are called function keys. They may appear across the top of the keyboard, or down the left-hand side. When instruction tells you to press the F12 key, it means for you to press one key that has this label on it; you will often see instructions such as press the F4 key, or press the F7 key.

Another important key is the one labeled ENTER. This is similar to the "Return" on a typewriter. Often you must press it to tell the computer you are ready for it to do something. For example, if you have finished typing a name and are ready for the computer to store it, or go and search for it, or to move to the next field so you can type a birth date, you often need to press the ENTER key.

Unlike a typewriter, you cannot use the small letter l for the number 1. The computer doesn't know what to do with this. You must use the number 1 from the row above the letters on the keyboard or number pad on the side. The same is true for the zero; you must use the zero rather than the letter O.

The keyboard is very sensitive. You need to barely touch the keys. If you are having trouble, it may be that you are holding a key down too long. It is possible to insert letters in the middle of a word or insert words in the middle of a sentence by using

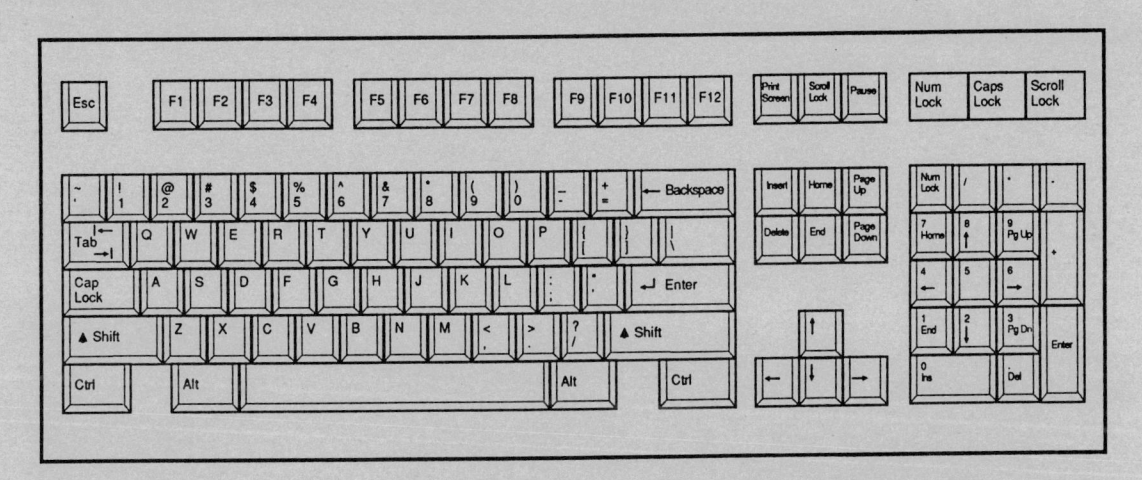

FIGURE 32 - A computer keyboard

the key labeled INSERT, or delete letters or words by using the key labeled DELETE.

You can move the "Cursor" (that little flashing line that tells you where the computer is going to begin action) by using the space bar, the small arrows on the side of the keyboard, the keys labeled PAGE UP or PAGE DOWN, or the key labeled BACK SPACE. (Find these keys on your keyboard and try each one of them.)

Don't be afraid of the computer. Contrary to what you may feel, you cannot hurt it (and it won't hurt you). Go ahead press the keys and become comfortable with making them do what you want to do. Experiment with them, and see what each one does.

Usually the key labeled ESC located on the left side of the top line of the keyboard will take you out of any program. Pressing it twice will usually take you back two steps.

Read the instructions that appear on the screen. These instructions will change from time to time, depending on the screen you are using. Read them carefully each time, and you will usually know what to do next.

Often the screen will present a question for you to answer, and the computer will not do anything until you answer the question. (Usually you answer by typing Y for yes or N for no.)

You do not need to know the difference between hardware and software to use a computer. However, the following descriptions may help you understand what others are talking about.

Hardware is the computer itself — what you see including the computer base, the monitor (screen), the keyboard. Inside it are "boards" (tiny computer components that store certain types of information.) Computers don't do anything without SOFTWARE to tell them what to do. Software is a program that tells the computer to do certain things and how to do them. Software is "loaded" into the computer's memory where the computer can follow the instructions in a particular program.

Before specific programs can work, the computer must have a basic software to tell it how to organize its space and make other software programs work. Among the earliest of these was Microsoft's disk operating system, or MS DOS. The more popular current systems are Windows 95 or Windows 98 or Windows NT. Macintosh has its own operating system which is different from either of these, and there is IBM's OS2 that was somewhat popular for a time. You begin with one of these, but until you have another software program on the computer, you still cannot do much on your computer. You need a word processor that will enable you to type letters or a genealogy software program such as Personal Ancestral File to allow you to organize your family history information. (While I refer to WordPerfect as the word processor I am most familiar with, Microsoft Word is another, and there are many others.)

A genealogy software program will allow you to type in names and dates and places and tell the computer what role each name fills in a family and have the computer link the names for you into pedigree charts and family groups. This detail can then be displayed or printed, or copied in computerized form.

Please note: You do not need a course in computers to use software programs. (Instructions with the software will tell you how to load the program onto your computer. However, you may want to have someone load the programs onto your computer for you.) Once the program is loaded onto your computer, all you need to do is read the instructions on the screen and follow them. Most programs also provide help messages (many do this by having you press the F1 function key). The user manual that comes with your program will tell you how to find these messages. Many publishers of software programs also provide telephone support to help their users.

Mostly, you just need to be brave enough to gain experience. FamilySearch programs (see page 44) include a tutorial for those who have never used a computer. It takes only about twenty minutes. Going through this can help you feel more comfortable using a computer.

B. Introduction to computers and family history/genealogy

Computers, as a part of our modern world, may at times frustrate or annoy us, but at other times they can make our tasks much easier to do. Family history is no exception. The use of computers is revolutionizing the way genealogy is done.

We will discuss three aspects of computer technology as it relates to family history or genealogy:

- Using computers to find genealogical information
- Using computers to organize and record your information
- Using computers to share your genealogy information

Computer technology is, of course, not limited to family history. It is being used to help store and retrieve information on all subjects. Genealogical detail is but one of the many types of information being automated and made more readily available for searches by using computers. The legal profession and the medical profession are among those using computers to enhance their access to the vast knowledge and resources available in their fields, and the same or similar technology is being applied to genealogy.

II. USING THE COMPUTER TO HELP YOU FIND INFORMATION

Using a computer to find genealogical information does not require that you have a computer in your home, or access to one in any other home. You can find the information in many libraries and use the computers there, then copy the information on paper (or sometimes on computer diskette, whichever you choose to use).

Some of the applications of computer technology in genealogy/family history include —

A. Library catalogs

Many libraries have computer-assisted access to the titles and descriptions of records they house.

The largest family history/genealogical library in the world, located in Salt Lake City, Utah, and its 3,000 Family History Centers (branches) throughout the world are no exception. Their Library Catalog is available for computer searching as part of FamilySearch, using compact discs. (See page 44 for more information on FamilySearch.)

This catalog allows you to type in the surname of a family and it will tell you how many titles the library has with that surname in the title or notes. Let's say you ask for the name Thompson, and it tells you it has 728 titles. Where do you begin?

The catalog will then allow you to put in two "key words" that can help you narrow your search: for example, let's say your Thompson family intermarried with the Drake surname, and they lived in South Carolina. By adding Drake and South Carolina, the computer will see how many of these titles contain one or both of these key words and you may narrow your search to only one or two titles. (Other Thompson books may contain information on your family, too, but this gives you the most likely ones for a beginning.)

You can also type in the names of places, and see all or selected records (such as births, marriages, deaths, military, history, genealogy) that are contained in that collection for each level of jurisdiction (such as town, county, and state or country). Each level will display a different set of records that were created by that particular jurisdiction — government, church, or some other organization.

Instructions appear on the screen, and help messages are available by pressing the F1 key. You must always go to the "full display" (press the F8 key) to obtain the call number of the record, which is required to locate the item in the main library or to order it for use at a Family History Center.

More detail is given to help you discover the records that may be most helpful to you and understand the information provided in the catalog entry in the Family History Library Catalog in the publication *Genealogy in the Computer Age: Understanding FamilySearch®*, volume 2 by Elizabeth L. Nichols (Family History Educators).

As computer technology changes, so will certain aspects of using a computerized catalog change. You may be able, for example, to type in any word that is found in the title or notes of a record and have the record retrieved. Watch for changes and be willing to learn about each new technique that is provided for your assistance.

Many Library Catalogs are now available on-line via the Internet. Each library catalog is unique, but all include instructions telling you what to do. And if you are in a library, there is usually a kind librarian to assist you when needed.

B. Genealogical computerized indexes and data files

An index gives brief information that will lead you to the full detail in the original source. Some genealogical indexes have been computerized.

Examples are the U.S. census indexes for 1850. These usually include only the name of the head of the household, the county within a state, and the page number of the original census record. These indexes may be available in book form, on microfiche, or by computer search for a fee. Some are now available on compact disc.

Another example of an index is the U.S. Social Security Death Index, which contains only one given name, the surname, the date of birth, and the date of death, the state where the Social Security number was issued, and the zip code of the person's legal address at the time of death. But the index can lead to names of relatives if you wish to pay the extra charge to obtain a copy of the full record. (See FamilySearch, page 44.)

The largest genealogical index in the world is published by the LDS Church and is titled the International Genealogical Index (IGI). (See FamilySearch, page 44.)

In addition to indexes, there are also available some genealogy computer databases that contain most or all of the pertinent facts or elements listed in the original record.

Recently released by The Church of Jesus Christ of Latter-day Saints are some computer databases that use Folio technology. Folio allows searches and retrieval without additional software. The software is part of the compact disc (CD). Released in 1998 are 1851 census records for three English counties: Devon, Norfolk, and Warwick. These are available on one compact disc from the LDS Distribution Center for $5.00.

SourceGuide®. Another type of software recently released by the LDS Church is known as the SourceGuide and introduces use of technology for instruction independent of genealogical data files. The SourceGuide provides quick and easy computer access to how-to knowledge compiled from the research and experience of many experts. The first release consists of research outlines or guides for each of the fifty U.S. states, the Canadian provinces, and major countries of the world. It also includes definitions of terms used in the research outlines, and catalog helps to guide you to the topics under which to look in the Family History Library Catalog to find the records that may contain the information you need. The actual records are not in SourceGuide, but only information about records.

The Family History Library call number is sometimes given for the more often used records, and you may be able to branch to a brief description of the record taken from the catalog entry that includes the details that will allow you to locate or order the item at a Family History Center.

SourceGuide is available on compact disc and can be purchased for use in your own home. The family history instruction is divided into three options from which you can choose and move back and forth as you study a locality: the how-to guides, word meanings, and catalog helper.

The how-to guides are research outlines which describe (a) the types of records available for each major geographical area, such as a U.S. state, (b) the time periods for which these records generally exist for that area, (c) where and how to find the records. (These research outlines have been previously available in paper form; many were updated and enlarged for the first release of the SourceGuide.)

Word meanings are definitions of terms used in the research outlines. These terms vary from commonly used ones such as "1920 United States census" or "'T' reference in Ireland householders index" (title allotment book entries) to foreign terms such as "Kyrkobocker, Sweden" (Swedish church records).

The catalog helper tells you what topics (subjects) to look under in the Family History Library Catalog to find the type of information you want for a specific place. For example, you may select New York for a locality and then a research goal such as death because you want to find a death record in the state of New York. Next click on *Step 3* and it will display the types of records in New York for you to search under when using the Family History Library Catalog, such as Vital Records, Cemeteries, Probate Records, Church Records, Obituaries, and then try Newspapers, Bible Records, Military Records, Town Records, Funeral Records.

In using SourceGuide, you can click on Help at the top of the screen and select "hide the help panel" and it will allow more space on the screen to display the text. This makes it much easier to read the information provided. You can select a place to search on. When that information is displayed some terms will be underlined. When you move the cursor to that term, a small hand will appear.

This tells you that more information is available by clicking on that term.

You can print marked selections or entire sections of an item. Select File from the upper corner of the screen, and then click on Print. For example, you may print a list of all of the guides (the shortest list is probably by author; the same author is listed for all of the guides, but it lists each guide in alphabetical order; five pages in the 1998 release. The list sorted by place is ten pages; it includes such items as each census worksheet, each area Family History Center address list, etc.). You can also print selections such as the catalog topics for death records of New York, or all catalog topics for the state of New York.

From the list of how-to guides, you can see a brief explanation of the contents of the guide. You can move to more information by clicking on the label "View How-to Guide" and then move to the definition of a term by clicking on any word that is underlined.

SourceGuide is now available from the LDS Church Distribution Center for $20.00. You can use it on your home computer (if you have sufficient computer memory and Windows 95). You do not need any additional software.

Other publishers are also providing more and more assistance via compact disc. Many of these can be purchased and used in your own home or at your library. One example of this is the Periodical Source Index, known as PERSI, compiled by the Allen County Public Library Genealogical Department and recently published on compact disc by Ancestry, Inc. This index is described as a comprehensive index of places, subjects, and surnames found in articles from a broad spectrum of English-language and French-Canadian genealogy and local history periodicals. It includes the general time period beginning in 1847 and is periodically updated. Check the dates on the copy you are using. PERSI does not include the actual articles, but tells you the name of the publication and the date and issue in which to find that article about a subject, place, or family.

Various genealogical publications now publish reviews of computer software and databases. One of these is the periodical *Genealogical Computing*, which occasionally publishes a listing of databases.

These ranged from the Ancestral File (see page 44) to an Index to Irish Householders (for time period about 1850), etc. Only Ancestral File and the International Genealogical Index (see below) listed more than one million records, and many are as small as 15,000 or less. These are representative. There are many more such files already in existence.

A publication to note is *Netting Your Ancestors: Genealogical Research on the Internet* by Cyndi Howells, published by Genealogical Publishing Company in Baltimore. This gives an excellent introduction to the Internet and its resources for family history.

Another type of database is one created by the Library of Congress. It is called American Memories. This is a computer file of pictures of certain places and time periods, including how the people dressed then. It can provide the setting for your ancestors' lives.

Database creation is a budding technology, and additional databases will be springing up everywhere. Check with your local genealogical society for current information.

C. Compact discs

Sometimes these computer databases are made available by printing the information in the form of books, sometimes in microfiche or microfilm, occasionally on-line, or sometimes using CD ROM (compact disc) technology (see below) and sometimes through all of these media.

One technology for making large databases of computerized information available to the public, without having the expense of on-line access but still having the ability to use the computer for retrieval, is known as compact disc (CD). Small compact discs will hold millions of records. These records can then be retrieved by using special computer software on a personal computer with a compact disc drive, which is standard equipment on most computers now. (These are similar to the CDs you buy in a music store.)

Information stored on a compact disc can be read but usually cannot be changed or added to. However, there are methods of making a copy of selected records that can then be copied to a diskette and used in your home computer. (See page 46.)

A leader in the field of making family history and genealogical information available by use of compact disc is The Church of Jesus Christ of Latter-day Saints (Mormons). They have published a set of computer programs and files using compact discs, grouped together under the name FamilySearch.

D. FamilySearch

FamilySearch is presently (May 1998) available in most of the 3,000 Family History Centers (branches of the Family History Library in Salt Lake City) scattered throughout the United States and Canada, and in many of those worldwide. It is not currently available for private purchase.

The major files presently available (May 1998) are:

- Ancestral File

    A pedigree-linked file for sharing genealogies, focusing on people who are now deceased. Anyone can use it or contribute records to it. It contains the information needed to display pedigree charts and family group records, and the names and addresses of those who submitted the information are attached to each record. The 1996 edition contained nearly 30 million names; the 1998 edition is expected to add millions more.

    There is no charge to use or to contribute to Ancestral File. (See overview on page 46.)

    When several descendants submit records for the same ancestor and the computer tries to bring together all of those records into one, there are sometimes problems. (Some records have more than 100 submitters.) It is suggested that you first see if your ancestors' records are in Ancestral File. If they are not, then add the information on them. And please proofread your records in your own file before submitting them to Ancestral File, as well as evaluate the information you may print or download from Ancestral File, since it may contain errors.

- To learn how you can submit your genealogical information to Ancestral File, in GEDCOM format, see page 61 under "Using computers to share your information."

- International Genealogical Index (IGI)

    The International Genealogical Index (IGI) contains millions of records of deceased persons. The 1997 release of the International Genealogical Index (IGI) contains the Main IGI, created in 1993, and an Addendum, which is periodically updated. The latest release in 1998 is 1997. The Main IGI plus the 1997 Addendum contain over 284 million names from more than 90 countries. This information comes from many different sources — some of them "extracted" (pertinent genealogical details copied) from original records of birth, christening, or marriage; and others from records prepared or compiled by relatives of those named. The batch number can be used to tell you whether an entry is from the extraction program. The prefix — first letter, numbers, or letter and number combination — is the key. Details are given in written instructions. There are about 100 million names from the Extraction Program in the IGI. It is important in using any entry from the IGI (as in most indexes) to determine the source of that particular entry. Some entries may not contain accurate information. The Main file (created in 1993) contains approximately 200 million names. Please note: the 1992 edition is the last available microfiche edition, although it does not contain millions of records that are available on compact disc. The microfiche edition contains only 187 million names (versus 284 million on computer).

    The IGI was not created as a research tool. It was created by the LDS Church for use by its members. This influences the way some things were computerized and indexed. However, the IGI is such a helpful index for anyone who wishes to do genealogical research that the LDS Church has made it available for others to use — free of charge. (Beginning with the 1997 release, there is no reference to LDS ordinance detail in the IGI. LDS Church members need to use the Ordinance Index.)

While names of parents or spouse are shown, their IGI records are not linked together. (However, the compact disc version of the IGI has a feature that allows you to search and display records based on the names of the parent(s), which often brings together records of possible brothers and sisters — depending on whether the names of the parents are listed exactly the same in the entries for each child.)

- U.S. Social Security Death Index, 1962-1996

An index made available by the U.S. Government as part of the Freedom of Information Act. It contains brief records of 50 million persons whose deaths were reported to the Social Security office, mostly between 1962-1996.

Information can also be copied from these data files, using a "GEDCOM" format (see page 61), taken home on a floppy diskette, and added to your records in your home computer, if you have a genealogy software program (such as PAF) that can handle GEDCOM files.

These FamilySearch data files (called resource files) are described in detail, with illustrations, in the 56-page publication *Genealogy in the Computer Age: Understanding FamilySearch®, volume 1: Ancestral File®, International Genealogical Index®, and Social Security Death Index, revised edition;* and *volume 2: The Personal Ancestral File® (PAF), the Family History Library Catalog™, More Resource Files, and Using Them All in Harmony,* by Elizabeth L. Nichols (Family History Educators).

The process of "downloading" or "exporting" (copying records found in these files), and "uploading" or "importing" (adding) them to your PAF database without retyping the information is also detailed in the above publications and will not be repeated here.

- Overview of how FamilySearch works:

1. Go to a library that has FamilySearch. (For a list of these libraries in your area, write to the Family History Library, 35 North West Temple Street, Salt Lake City, UT 84150 or check the Internet at www.lds.org. *Note:* be sure you use .org as the last item, or you will not get the LDS Church.) The SourceGuide also has the addresses of Family History Centers. You may have to schedule a time in advance when you can use FamilySearch for a specified period of time (perhaps 30 minutes or one hour).

2. Select the file you wish to use from a menu presented. (For this example, we will select Ancestral File.)

3. Type in the name of a deceased person of interest to you. (The year of birth is optional but helpful, especially for common names such as John Smith.)

4. Press the F12 key to begin the search.

5. The computer will tell you which compact disc to insert in the disc player or drive. (Some large centers have their discs on a network, and you do not need to insert a disc.) The computer screen will then display an alphabetical list of the records available, showing you the name; year of birth; state, country, or for some areas the county of birth; and usually the name of a relative (father if that is listed in the file; otherwise the spouse). By pressing the ENTER key, for the name highlighted you can see names of both parents and the spouse (if these records are in the file and linked to this person's record).

6. With the highlight on the name of interest to you, choose from the options across the top of the screen: to see a pedigree chart, press the F7 key; to see a family group record, press the F6 key); for a list of names and addresses of those who submitted the information, press the F9 key and then select submitters.

The computer will prompt you when to change discs and which disc to insert in the CD drive.

7. Choose how you want to copy the

information you find. There are three choices:

- Make a printed copy of a pedigree chart, family group record, or list of submitters.

- Make a copy of the automated data on a diskette that can be used on your home computer to use with a word processor (called an ASCII file).

- Make a copy of the automated data that you can take home and use in your home computer using a genealogy software program, such as PAF (or some other software that handles GEDCOM format records). You will not need to retype the information but can import (upload) it into your computer. (See page 61.)

Note: It takes time to download or copy information from these files, so plan wisely the use of your time when you schedule use of FamilySearch. You may need to look at them one time, and go back another time to obtain a GEDCOM copy of the records; or to obtain only four or five generations the first time, and take it home and experiment with it, then go back again to copy more records.

8. Take the diskette home and add the information to your PAF database (or other genealogy software program that handles GEDCOM records).

Note: You may want to put them in a temporary file and study them before adding them to your regular file. You can then run the "Possible Problem Report" and keep from importing problems into your own personal database.

9. When you are at the FamilySearch workstation, to correct errors in the information in Ancestral File, you can press a different function key (F3), and change or add the information. You must have the correct information with you at the FamilySearch work station. (Instructions are presented on the screen.) You will not change the information on the compact disc, but your correction will be saved on a diskette, which you then send to Ancestral File, 50 East North Temple Street, Salt Lake City, UT 84150. It will be processed with other submissions and corrections, and the most recent information will be displayed in a future edition of Ancestral File. All corrections and changes will appear in a "Change History" report for that record.

Note: If a field in an Ancestral File record already has information, the only way you can correct it is by using this edit feature on a FamilySearch computer or by making a PAF version 3.0 submission. If the field is blank, you can add to it by submitting an additional record for that person. For example, if the birth field says "about 1714" and you know that the person was born 14 Jun 1715, you will need to change that information using the edit function at a FamilySearch work station. But if the birth field is blank, you can add the birth date either by using the F3 edit function at a FamilySearch work station or by submitting an additional record for that person, with other family members, so the computer can match and merge the records.

- Other programs and files in FamilySearch

1. Family History Library Catalog (see page 41). The catalog is a bibliographical database, describing the books and other records in the library's vast holdings. It does not contain all of the names from those records. Its purpose is to provide a description of each record and the call number so you can locate that particular record.

2. Personal Ancestral File® (PAF). A program for recording and organizing your genealogical data (See pages 50, 74).

3. Scottish Church Records. Ten millions records taken from early Scottish Church records. (Over 50% of these are also in the International Genealogical Index [IGI].)
4. U.S. Military Records. Two data files limited to records of U.S. citizens who died or were reported dead during the Korean and Vietnam conflicts. Both files originated from the U.S. government.
5. LDS Options, which is an item that appears on some FamilySearch menus, such as those located in LDS meetinghouses and Family History Centers. Within the LDS Options are found:

    TempleReady, a program for helping LDS members submit names for Church ordinances in the temple (see page 23) and the Ordinance Index (see page 73).

E. Electronic media

When we refer to electronic media, we are going to discuss electronic mail (e-mail), newsgroups, and the Internet.

Electronic mail, known as e-mail, is a means of sending written messages over the phone line, using a modem that will allow it to be sent or received within your computer. You can then read it on the computer, print it, reply to it, and file it or delete it. You can also send data files using e-mail. An address book within your e-mail program allows you to easily keep e-mail addresses and to send letters without having to type the address each time.

In addition to the modem (which is standard equipment on most computers now) you must have a carrier. Large national companies such as CompuServe, America Online, and Prodigy include e-mail with other electronic services, for a fee. Other types of service are more limited in scope. For example, one completely free company that handles just e-mail is Juno which can be reached at http://www.juno.com or by phone at 1-800-654-5866 (in 1998).

Once you have e-mail, you may enjoy receiving and sending mail from and to anywhere in the world.

You may also receive unwanted mail, sometimes not appropriate for clean-minded persons. Delete them immediately; you don't have to read them.

- Introduction to the Internet

    We have heard about the Internet, but what does it have to do with family history? You do not have to use the Internet to do family history, but it is one of many resources that may provide valuable help to you in this field of study. However, do not expect the Internet to change the basic skills and tasks required to compile an accurate genealogy. It is only another tool to help in this process.

    The Internet, simply put, is composed of many computer networks located anywhere in the world that are linked together and with which you can communicate. You must have a modem in order to access the Internet. A modem is necessary to participate in any way in the electronic exchange of information. A modem links your computer to others by using your phone line. You can still use your phone line for regular telephone calls, except when you are connected via modem to other computers (sending or receiving e-mail or using the Internet). To access the Internet, you must also have a Browser of some kind. This comes with most computers now. Two commonly used ones are Netscape Navigator and Microsoft Internet Explorer. This may be incorporated into your computer without your having to do anything. Then you must have a connection with the Internet. You can do this through local facilities or through one of the larger national facilities. Either one can connect you with people all over the world. For example, CompuServe, America Online, and Prodigy are companies where for a specified fee you can access the Internet, and some telephone companies are now entering the field. There are different packages you can subscribe to. One may include up to five hours per month for a specified fee, while another gives you unlimited hours for a larger fee. The software often comes unrequested in the mail, or you can contact the company and ask for a free trial. This allows you to use it free for a specified period, usually up to a month or a certain number of hours. What you use will depend on your needs and your resources. Local companies also offer these services. All provide ways to easily access their services and the Internet, as well as e-mail exchange.

The format of electronic addresses may seem strange, and it is important to have each letter and punctuation mark (such as slash, dot) just as given in the address. The first letters for Internet addresses are "http" which stand for Hyper Text Transfer Protocol. These are followed by two forward slashes and a colon, and the letters "www" for Worldwide Web, which is a network of electronic sites called web pages. The www is followed by a dot (or period); leave no blank spaces. Most addresses require all lowercase letters. The ending of the site address is dependent upon the type of site it is. For example, *.gov* means government; *.com* means commercial; *.edu* means education; *.org* means an organization.

Most Internet-access software already displays the first part of a worldwide web address, and you can just add the specific details of the last part of the address, and then proofread it. Once you have visited a place, you can usually put that address in your "favorite places" file (or some similar name) which can be accessed as a menu item on your computer screen, and thereafter you can access that web page by simply clicking on that listing.

Move around an Internet screen by using your mouse. You can usually move to additional detail by clicking the mouse wherever a hand appears on the screen. The hand-shaped cursor indicates a link to another place on this Internet site or to another site. Often, underlined text in another color also indicates a link. There is usually a way to go back one page by clicking on a button on the screen. Its exact title will vary. There is some type of "search" or "find" option for you to fill in. It is possible to print pages either using a visible button on the screen or by use of the FILE menu, and find PRINT, or copy and paste. It is also often possible to download copies of files, sometimes free but usually for a cost.

Many places that you could visit on the Internet can only be visited if you subscribe, though some offer an introductory visit for free. You can also shop via the Internet, participate in chat groups, create listings on your genealogy needs, or read and respond to queries posted by others.

- Some Places You May Want to Visit

USGenWeb. This site contains a Web page for every county in the United States. The information provided varies, but gives helpful details about doing research in that specific area. It is possible in most of them to communicate with the host for that "Web page" and find out how you can post queries to it. Its address is: http://www.usgenweb.org. (Remember: all lowercase letters, include the colon, the forward slashes, the periods [except for the one following com, which simply ends the sentence] and no blank spaces.) Once you are at the general site, you can choose the specific state and then the county of interest to you. You can, of course, visit more than one county if you wish. You can print selected text from the information given.

You can find the address of the nearest LDS Family History Center on the Web page for the LDS Church at www.lds.org (be very careful to note that this address ends with .org. Any other ending will not take you to this site.) There are also many Library Catalogs available via the Internet. And some sites that allow you to download genealogical details (versus information about what may exist or how to obtain it). What is available and the address of how to reach it may change quickly on the Internet, as in other modes of communication.

There are many exchanges of GEDCOM files possible via the Internet. While this can give you valuable information and clues, many of these do not include any source citations. Therefore they must be treated with caution. Just because the information is automated and available via the Internet (or any other way) does not guarantee that it is correct. If no sources are listed, you will need to verify it. Mistakes are often made in pedigrees that will link you into an incorrect family and pedigree.

Cyndi's List. Another site you will want to visit is known as Cyndi's List of Genealogy Sites on the Internet. Her current address (1998) is: http://www.cyndislist.com. She has brought together information on thousands of web sites that may be of interest to genealogists.

- Search engines

  A tool to help you find places you may wish to visit is known as a "Search engine." These identify many genealogy places of interest including beginner's guides, surnames, and ethnic resources.

  Popular search engines include:
  Excite!   http://www/excite.com
  Alta Vista http://www.altavista.com
  Infoseek   http://www.infoseek.com
  Yahoo!   http://www.yahoo.com

- Newsgroups and Bulletin Boards

  Newsgroups are discussion groups where you can join as an observer or participant. You may also post queries, respond to those posted by others, download copies of what is there, have copies automatically sent to you via e-mail for certain selected surnames or topics, etc. There are many of these on the subject of genealogy. You can usually locate one within your carrier by typing the word *genealogy*, or by using a search engine.

  Many organizations, such as the National Genealogical Society, maintain a bulletin board that provides information about its services and products. They may also have web sites that you can visit.

  There are usually many options available to you on computer newsgroups and bulletin boards. Some must be checked each day as they are only left up for a day or two while others are posted for longer periods. You may also participate in conferences on selected topics, or just "talk" with others interested in family history (by typing your messages on your computer keyboard and having them displayed on the screen for all participants to see). Unless you are in the same telephone calling area, there will be the cost of the long distance call, unless this is included in your carrier's package (which it usually is in a commercial carrier). However, it is still often necessary to pay to participate, whether by joining the group or subscribing to a service.

Use of electronic services may be very helpful and may speed up your access to needed information in genealogy. It may quickly put you in touch with someone who has the very information that you need. You can also create your own web page and invite others to visit it. You can spend a great amount of time in reading what is going on (some of it wasted time). But it will not replace the tasks required in compiling accurate genealogies nor the need to carefully evaluate what you find by this means. Use it, but don't be intimidated by information found via the Internet. Like all other sources, the quality of what you get will vary and must be evaluated and used with wisdom.

III. USING COMPUTERS TO ORGANIZE AND RECORD YOUR INFORMATION

Note: If you are new to use of computers, see page 39.

A. Equipment you must have

To record your genealogy using a computer, you must have:

- Access to a personal computer (also called a home computer). This is the hardware.

- Access to a genealogy program that will link records into families and pedigrees. This is the software.

(*Note:* Most Genealogy software programs require that you have a disk operating system [DOS] and Windows [3.1, 95, 98, NT] loaded before they will work. The version of DOS needs to be updated occasionally.)

There are many genealogy software programs from which to choose. These programs vary greatly in price and in functionality (what they can do). The most expensive is not always the most functional.

Among the more popular programs is one called Personal Ancestral File or PAF. It is available to anyone for $15 from the Salt Lake City Distribution Center, 1191 West 1700 South, Salt Lake City, UT 84104. The most recent version as of May 1998 is 3.0 which is a DOS program but can work well with Windows. You can get the MS DOS version (which works on IBM and compatible computers) or 2.31 for the Macintosh. Although PAF does not have a Windows version, the MS DOS version usually works well with either Windows 3.1 or Windows 95. And with the introduction of the Personal Ancestral File Companion, which is a Windows program that interfaces with PAF 3.0 and allows you to print quality pedigree charts, family groups, and other reports, it works out well.

In one survey made by *Genealogical Computing* (a periodical) more computer users listed Personal Ancestral File (PAF) as their choice of genealogy software programs than any other software. In addition, this program is inexpensive, easily available, created to share computerized information as well as record and print it, and this author is most familiar with it; therefore, we will use this program as a basis for our discussion in this publication.

This is not to indicate that other programs are not good, and one of them may suit your needs better than this program.

B. **The basics of what you do**
- With any genealogy software program, you would do the following, but some details will vary:
1. Prepare a file to hold your information. This may be on the hard disk or on a diskette.
2. Type the information into the computer. This requires that you type certain "elements" (names, dates, places) into specified spaces, called "fields."

```
┌═INDIVIDUAL RECORD═══════════════════════════════════════════════════┐
│                                                                      │
│       Given Name:                                                    │
│          Surname:                                                    │
│              Sex:            Title:                                  │
│  ──────────────────────────────────────────────────────────────────  │
│       Birth Date:                                                    │
│            Place:                                                    │
│                                                                      │
│ Christening Date:                                                    │
│            Place:                                                    │
│                                                                      │
│       Death Date:                                                    │
│            Place:                                                    │
│                                                                      │
│      Burial Date:                                                    │
│            Place:                                                    │
│                                                                      │
│                                                    ID Number:       │
│  ──────────────────────────────────────────────────────────────────  │
│    Date record was last changed:                   RIN:              │
│  Date submitted to Ancestral File:                 AFN:              │
└──────────────────────────────────────────────────────────────────────┘
 Esc=Cancel   F1=Save    F3=Notes   F4=Sources    F8=Ditto      Alt+H=Help
```

FIGURE 33 - PAF data entry screen, blank

```
┌─INDIVIDUAL RECORD════════════════════════════════════════════╗
│                                                              │
│      Given Name: Harrison Harris (Harry)                     │
│        Surname: Nichols                                      │
│            Sex: M         Title: (TWIN)                      │
├──────────────────────────────────────────────────────────────┤
│     Birth Date: 24 Sep 1859                                  │
│          Place: Starks,Somerset,Maine                        │
│                                                              │
│Christening Date:                                             │
│          Place:                                              │
│                                                              │
│     Death Date: 27 Apr 1940                                  │
│          Place: South Bend,St. Joseph,IN                     │
│                                                              │
│    Burial Date:                                              │
│          Place: Ladysmith,Rusk,WI                            │
│                                                              │
│                                            ID Number:        │
├──────────────────────────────────────────────────────────────┤
│   Date record was last changed:            RIN: 18           │
│ Date submitted to Ancestral File:          AFN: 2TFB-DK      │
│                                         There are notes/sources │
└──────────────────────────────────────────────────────────────┘
 Esc=Cancel   F1=Save    F3=Notes    F4=Sources   F8=Ditto              Alt+H=Help
```

FIGURE 33A - PAF data entry screens, filled out

Note: You can also add records to your computer file without having to type them in, if someone else has typed them into a computer. (See page 41, "Using the computer to help you find information," and page 61, "Using the computer to share genealogical information" for details.)

3. Link the individuals into families.

    The computer will do this for you, if you tell it what position or role the person fills in that family (for example, father, mother, child). See figure 35.

    The computer automatically assigns every record an identification number. Some programs allow the user to see and use this number. On these PAF screens, it is called the RIN (record identification number).

    The computer also assigns a number to every family. On these screens this family number is called the MRIN (marriage record identification number).

    You can link the records into families at the time you type the information into the computer, or you can retrieve a record that you have previously typed and link it into a family later.

    Example: You typed your record into the computer and linked it as a husband or wife with your spouse and children to create a family unit.

```
┌──────────────────────────────────────────────────────────────────────────┐
│ MARRIAGE RECORD FOR Harrison Harris Harry NICHOLS/Mabel Louise FARWELL  │
├──────────────────────────────────────────────────────────────────────────┤
│      Date:                                                               │
│     Place:                                                               │
│                                              Divorced? (Y/N):            │
├──────────────────────────────────────────────────────────────────────────┤
│ Esc=Cancel   F1=Save   F3=Notes   F4=Sources   F8=Ditto    Alt+H=Help    │
└──────────────────────────────────────────────────────────────────────────┘
```

FIGURE 34 - A marriage detail screen, PAF 3.0

```
            IDENTIFY HUSBAND
  Husband is not yet in the file. Add him.
  Husband is in the file. Select from list.
  Husband is in the file. I know RIN.
  Husband is in the file. I do not know RIN.
  Husband is not known.

↓↑=Move      Enter=Select      Esc=Cancel      Alt+H=Help
```

FIGURE 35 - *Menu listing options for linking names into a family*

Now you have typed in names of your parents, and you want to link your record to theirs in the role of a child.

You can do this by retrieving the record already typed. If you know the RIN, you can retrieve it by typing in this number (see the third item on the menu in figure 35). If you do not know the RIN, you can type in the name (and other details if you choose), and retrieve the record in that way (see the fourth item in figure 35). Or you can choose to select from the alphabetical list of all of the names in your file.

Note: If you forgot and typed in the record again, PAF allows you to match and merge the two records, thus retaining the links of both records to descendants and to ancestors. (See pages 55-56 for more information about match/merge.) Many programs require that you delete one record, and then you must link the remaining record as either a spouse or a child.

When you have typed in your father's parents' records, you will also need to link your father to them as a child. Use whatever method your software tells you to use. PAF allows you to do this by pressing A for add and selecting from the menu. (See figure 38.)

You can also add another child by selecting that option (or change the order of the children listed by pressing G for rearrange).

4. Display the records you have typed, showing them linked into pedigrees and family groups.

Each software program will tell you how to get to this display. For example, in PAF you get to this display when the program first comes up in a file.

If you want to see more generations

```
══SMALL PEDIGREE - ELN═══════════════════════════════════════════════════════
                                        ┌─ Elijah D. NICHOLS-6
  Harrison Harris Harry NICHOLS-18      │    7 Jan 1820                      ►
  24 Sep 1859                           ┤    Anson,Somerset,Maine
  Starks,Somerset,Maine                 │                          MRIN:  8
     (Other marriages)                  │
     MARRIAGE:22 Oct 1889    MRIN: 7    └─ Betsey Ann MORSE-20
  Mabel Louise FARWELL-19                    14 May 1836                    ►
  30 Dec 1861                                Starks,Somerset,Maine
  Greene,Androscoggin,Maine

 ─CHILDREN──────────────────────────────────────Born───Parent Link──────────
    1.Veva Mae NICHOLS-90                       1890
    2.Harold Farwell NICHOLS-91                 1892
  ◄ 3.Leta Claire NICHOLS-92                    1893
    4.Avis Ursie NICHOLS-93                     1895
    5.Zella Margie NICHOLS-94                   1897
    6.Nona Marie NICHOLS-95                     1899
  ◄ 7.Clyde Redmond NICHOLS [Sr]-4              1902
  Enter to add

  ─────────────────────────────────────────────────────────────────────────
  Options:  Edit       1=name list     Rin    Print   F3=notes      F6=more options
            Add        2=indiv browse  mriN   Large   F5=open file  Esc=Exit
      ↑↓→   Delete     3=show family   searcH                       Alt+H=Help
```

FIGURE 36 - *The Small Pedigree screen displays three generations (PAF 3.0)*

The Genesis of Your Genealogy

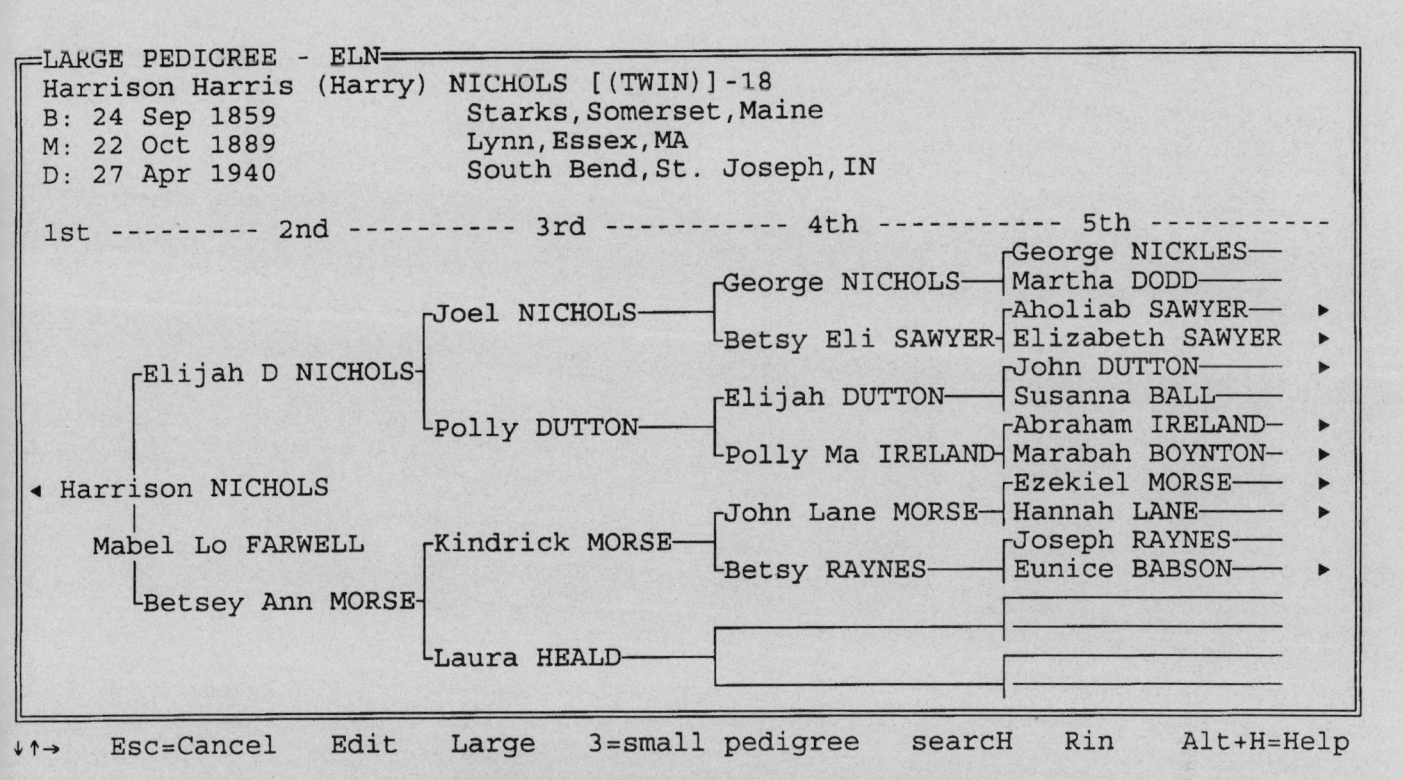

```
==LARGE PEDIGREE - ELN==
 Harrison Harris (Harry) NICHOLS [(TWIN)]-18
 B: 24 Sep 1859          Starks,Somerset,Maine
 M: 22 Oct 1889          Lynn,Essex,MA
 D: 27 Apr 1940          South Bend,St. Joseph,IN

 1st --------- 2nd ---------- 3rd ----------- 4th ----------- 5th -----------
                                                            ┌─George NICKLES──
                                            ┌─George NICHOLS┤ Martha DODD─────
                          ┌─Joel NICHOLS────┤               ┌─Aholiab SAWYER──  ▸
                          │                 └─Betsy Eli SAWYER┤Elizabeth SAWYER ▸
         ┌─Elijah D NICHOLS┤                                 ┌─John DUTTON─────  ▸
         │                │                 ┌─Elijah DUTTON──┤ Susanna BALL────
         │                └─Polly DUTTON────┤                ┌─Abraham IRELAND─  ▸
         │                                  └─Polly Ma IRELAND┤Marabah BOYNTON─  ▸
 ◂ Harrison NICHOLS                                           ┌─Ezekiel MORSE──  ▸
                                            ┌─John Lane MORSE─┤Hannah LANE─────  ▸
         Mabel Lo FARWELL ┌─Kindrick MORSE──┤                ┌─Joseph RAYNES───
                          │                 └─Betsy RAYNES───┤ Eunice BABSON──  ▸
         └─Betsey Ann MORSE┤
                          │
                          └─Laura HEALD─────
 ↓↑→   Esc=Cancel    Edit    Large    3=small pedigree    searcH    Rin    Alt+H=Help
```

FIGURE 37 - *A five-generation pedigree chart*

of your pedigree, in PAF, while on the small pedigree screen, press the letter "L" (for large) to see five generations displayed.

Any software will allow you to do a number of functions, depending on which key you press. In PAF, from the same "small pedigree" screen, you can view the full genealogical detail plus the notes, or the marriage detail, edit (change) information, or add records of additional family members all by following the instructions on the bottom of the screen.

```
┌─────────────────────────────────────────┐
│      WHAT DO YOU WANT TO ADD?           │
│                                         │
│  Add Spouse                             │
│  Add Parents                            │
│  Add Child                              │
│  Add New Individual Not Yet in File     │
│  Add New Family Not Yet in File         │
├─────────────────────────────────────────┤
│ ↓↑=Move  Enter=Select  Esc=Cancel  Alt+H=Help │
└─────────────────────────────────────────┘
```

FIGURE 38 - *To Add records, first select the role of the person in this family*

5. Search and retrieve records

You can search for any name in the database. Each system is different. But most allow similar retrieval methods by name, by relationship, by record identification number, by family number, etc.

For example, in PAF, begin in the Small Pedigree screen as shown in figure 36, and press the letter H to have a blank screen displayed for you to type in the information on which you wish to search (such as Veva Nichols).

Or you can move other names into the principal pedigree position by simply typing the letter of the relationship (F for Father, M for Mother, S for spouse, C plus number if more than one child) for child.

Type R and then the RIN to retrieve a record by the record identification number. Or type N and then the MRIN (marriage record identification number or family number) of the couple you want displayed.

When you search by name, you can add as much or as little detail as you wish. For example, if you have only

```
┌─NAME LIST - ELN════════════════╗  ┌──────────────────────────────────────┐
│                                 │  │  Name:  NICHOLS,Harrison Harris Harry-18
│   NICHOLS,HarrietHattie Harr  ↑ │  │  Sex:   M            ID Num:
│   NICHOLS,Harrison Harris Ha    │  │                      AFN: 2TFB-DK
│   NICHOLS,Harry Leroy           │  │ Birth:  24 Sep 1859
│   NICHOLS,Harry Redmond         │  │ Place:  Starks,Somerset,Maine
│   NICHOLS,Jacob Harrison        │  │   Chr:
│   NICHOLS,James V. W.           │  │ Place:
│   NICHOLS,Jane Louise           │  │ Death:  27 Apr 1940
│   NICHOLS,Jared Scott           │  │ Place:  South Bend,St. Joseph,IN
│   NICHOLS,Jenalyn               │  │ Burial:
│   NICHOLS,Joel                  │  │ Place:  Ladysmith,Rusk,WI
│   NICHOLS,Joel Bolton           │  │
│   NICHOLS,John                  │  │
│   NICHOLS,John                  │  │
│   NICHOLS,Jonathan Ross         │  │ Father: NICHOLS,Elijah D.-6
│   NICHOLS,Julie Linn            │  │ Mother: MORSE,Betsey Ann-20
│   NICHOLS,Karen Rebecca         │  │ Spouse: FARWELL,Mabel Louise-19
│   NICHOLS,Kenneth Murray        │  │ Spouse: COOK,Mabel-1305
│   NICHOLS,Kermit Bolton         │  │ Spouse:
│   NICHOLS,Lesa Ann            ↓ │  │
└─────────────────────────────────┘  └──────────────────────────────────────┘
Options:  Edit    searcH    3=Small Pedigree            Esc=Cancel  Alt+H=Help
```

FIGURE 38A - *Sect a name from the alphabetical list*

one record in the file by the name of Veva, only type that name; if you have many records for different persons named John Harvie, you may want to add at least a birth year, or a locality to your search.

The computer will retrieve the first record it comes to that contains that name, and display it for you, with the question on the screen asking if this is the one you want. You always have the chance to say yes or no. You can also browse the alphabetical name list.

You can usually search on a locality, if you wish. Type in *Charlotte, NC* in the locality fields, and the computer will retrieve records containing that word or combination of words.

Note: Most computer programs will retrieve only records that are spelled exactly as you typed the word. You cannot type NC this time, and N.C. next time, and North Carolina next time, and have the computer retrieve all of these; it will only retrieve the ones that are stored in the computer as you typed your request. This is also true of names of persons.

Some programs allow you to also retrieve information from the notes. Read your instruction manual. PAF, for example, provides for this type of search as part of the FOCUS function.

6. Edit (correct, modify, change, delete, merge). Any genealogical software program designed to record and organize your information will provide some way for you to make changes in the data. Often this is possible in a variety of ways.

For example, in PAF, you can—

– From the Small Pedigree screen, edit individual detail by pressing ENTER when the name whose record you want to change appears in the principal position on the screen (see page 52); or marriage detail by highlighting Marriage, then pressing ENTER.

– When you have two records for the same person in the file, merge these records into one by using the match/merge function in PAF. (This retains the links in

```
==MERGE TWO INDIVIDUALS=====================================================
┌─Merge-Into═══════════════════════════╗┌─Merge-From═══════════════════════════╗
│   Name: Harrison Harris Ha NICHOLS-18 ││   Name: Harry NICHOLS-3420            │
│    Sex: M                             ││    Sex: M                             │
│  Birth: 24 Sep 1859                   ││  Birth: 1859                          │
│  Place: Starks,Somerset,Maine         ││  Place: Maine                         │
│    Chr:                               ││    Chr:                               │
│  Place:                               ││  Place:                               │
│  Death: 27 Apr 1940                   ││  Death: 27 Apr 1940                   │
│  Place: South Bend,St. Joseph,IN      ││  Place:                               │
│ Burial:                               ││ Burial:                               │
│  Place: Ladysmith,Rusk,WI             ││  Place: Ladysmith,Rusk,Wisconsin      │
│                                       ││                                       │
│                                       ││                                       │
│                                       ││                                       │
│ Father: Elijah D. NICHOLS-6           ││ Father:                               │
│ Mother: Betsey Ann MORSE-20           ││ Mother:                               │
│ Spouse: Mabel Louise FARWELL-19       ││ Spouse: Mabel Louise FARWELL-2755     │
│ Spouse: Mabel COOK-1305               ││ Spouse:                               │
│ Spouse:                               ││ Spouse:                               │
│  ID No:            AFN: 2TFB-DK       ││  ID No:            AFN:               │
└═══════════════════════════════════════┘└═══════════════════════════════════════┘
Options: Edit    Print     F3=Notes      1-parent's family  3-marriages   Esc=Cancel
         !merge  Switch    next Match    2-other parents    Find          Alt+H=Help
```

FIGURE 39 - Two records ready to be merged in PAF 3.0

both records, which deleting a record does not do.) See figure 39 for an example of merging a record in PAF.

– Delete a record, a family, or a group of records.

– *Note:* Deleting a family will remove all records for all individuals. You may just want to unlink the family members. This is called "removing" a person from that role in that family, such as removing a child from its link to these parents. The record then still remains in your database. To remove the record from your data file, select Delete.

```
╔══════════════════════════════════════╗
║      WHAT DO YOU WANT TO DELETE?     ║
╠══════════════════════════════════════╣
║ Delete Individual                    ║
║ Delete Range of Individuals          ║
║ Delete All Family Members            ║
║ Delete Individual Notes              ║
║ Remove Individual as a Child         ║
║ Remove Individual as a Parent        ║
║ Remove Family Links                  ║
╚══════════════════════════════════════╝
```

FIGURE 39A - Delete and remove are separate functions but found under the same menu option

– Change or delete information in the notes (see page 54).

– Match/merge two records for the same person.

– Match/merge is an extremely helpful feature. In PAF, you can select that option by pressing T (listed on the second menu, found by pressing first F6). You then have the choice to let the computer retrieve records that it thinks may be duplicate (automatic match/merge). Both records are displayed on the screen, and you can decide if you think they are duplicate records for the same person. If you do, press the exclamation point (shift-key plus the number 1 at the same time). The basic information on the left of the screen is retained. If there is information on the right that is not on the left, then it is added. If you want the basic information from the record on the right, you can switch the records by pressing the letter S. Or you can edit the record on the left.

- If you prefer, print out a copy of possible duplicate records, and choose the option to match two records. Then type in the RIN for the two records (they are listed on your printout of possible duplicates) and merge them in the same way, or select the option to choose the record highlighted when you began the match/merge process for the first record, and choose the second record by RIN, name, or by selecting it from the list.

Note: There is another option that allows records with the same Ancestral File number (AFN) to be automatically merged, with no effort on your part. This is designed primarily for handling duplication of records in downloads from Ancestral File, when you download records at different times and have overlap. (See page 60 for more information).

There may be a caution needed in merging records. When you merge two records for the same person that have different places, you may have problems. For example, one record lists William Warner as born Stonington, , CT (no county listed, but there is a blank field where the county should go). The other record lists him as "of Spafford, Onondaga, NY." You want to preserve the basic information given in the record that refers to his exact birthplace, which is listed as Stonington, , Connecticut. But the program may fill in the missing county causing your merged record to list Stonington as being in Onondaga County, CT, which is false. You will need to edit such records, and delete the name of the county or replace it with New London, which is the correct county for Stonington, CT. (If both records have complete names of town, county, and state [or equivalents], this is not a problem.)

7. Print

To print pedigree charts, family group records, index lists, and other reports,

---

```
AHNENTAFEL CHART FOR CLYDE REDMOND NICHOLS [SR] - RLN.PAF              21 Apr 1998   Page  1 of  1
=====================================================================================================

                                          1st GENERATION

  1 Clyde Redmond NICHOLS [Sr]-4: b 28 Jul 1902  Phillips,Price,Wisconsin; m 27 Mar 1928  Cambria,Montgomery,VA;
    d 26 Mar 1979  Charlotte,Mecklenburg,North Carolina
-----------------------------------------------------------------------------------------------------
                                          2nd GENERATION

  2 Harrison Harris (Harry) NICHOLS [(TWIN)]-18: b 24 Sep 1859  Starks,Somerset,Maine; m 22 Oct 1889  Lynn,Essex,
    MA; d 27 Apr 1940  South Bend,St. Joseph,IN
  3 Mabel Louise FARWELL-19: b 30 Dec 1861  Greene,Androscoggin,Maine;  d  3 Mar 1946  Ladysmith,Rusk,WI
-----------------------------------------------------------------------------------------------------
                                          3rd GENERATION

  4 Elijah D. NICHOLS-6: b  7 Jan 1820  Anson,Somerset,Maine; m  5 Mar 1857  Starks,Somerset,ME; d 28 Jan 1878
    Starks,Somerset,ME
  5 Betsey Ann MORSE-20: b 14 May 1836  Starks,Somerset,Maine; d 17 Sep 1914  Detroit,Somerset,ME
  6 John Milton FARWELL-10: b 22 Sep 1833  Greene,Kennebec,ME; m  3 Jul 1859  Greene,Androscoggin,ME; d 17 Jul
    1866  Winthrop,Kennebec,ME
  7 Eliza Kent STEVENS-55: b 24 Sep 1842  Winthrop,Kennebec,Maine; d 25 Jul 1892  Winthrop,Kennebec,Maine
```

FIGURE 44 - An Ahnentafel Chart, a type of pedigree chart.

you must have a printer connected to your computer. A variety of reports can be printed, called "printouts."

You can choose to print a single pedigree chart, a single family group record, a single summary of the information on a particular person (includes genealogical detail and notes for an individual or excluding notes), or a group of charts.

You can print a variety of special reports. For example, PAF has a special "Possible Problem Report" that helps you identify errors in dates, such as transposing a year. It will tell you if the person is listed as dying before he was born, or if there are too many years between the years of birth of the husband and wife (one born in 1709 and one in 1911 — obviously a typing error of one record), less than nine months between births of children, etc. (This is found under *P* for print and *lists* in PAF.)

You may have the option of how many generations of your pedigree you want to show on your pedigree chart. And you may be able to tell the computer to print a specified number of generations (say 9), automatically extending to additional pedigree charts, and have the computer add all cross-references to extending pedigree charts (this person is also found on chart 10; this is the same as person no. 8 on chart 1). And you can print an alphabetical index of the names on your pedigree, and include or omit printing the supporting family group records.

Or you may choose to print a "range" of family group records or individual records. You can do this by identifying the RIN numbers (record identification numbers) for individual records, such as 1-9, 15, 18, 34.

You can print lists of the record identification numbers or the family numbers by requesting printouts, arranged either chronologically or in alphabetical order.

You can choose to have a pedigree chart printed down the page instead of across it, which is useful at certain times.

– You can choose to include or exclude certain items on your printouts, such as RINs, notes, additional marriages, LDS ordinance dates. (See page 22 for more information on LDS needs.)

– *Note:* Some of these choices are made from the Utility menu, while others are made from the regular menus or by answering questions presented on the screen. Consult your instruction book with your software program.

– You may also be able to use your word processor in connection with your genealogy software program.

Your word processor can also be used for address lists, correspondence, and other things that will help with your genealogy. There are also many "add-on" programs available for sale that increase the options of things you can do with your data, once it is typed into the computer.

8. Notes and sources

Sources refer to where you obtained the information. Notes can be anything you wish to include such as biographical information, explanation of discrepancies, occupations, church affiliations, honors received, or good deeds done. In version 2.31 and earlier, PAF had only the capacity to record notes, which had to include your source citations. Beginning with version 3.0, these are separate functions. In PAF 3.0, the sources will be included in Ancestral File downloads, while the notes are not intended to be.

Some GEDCOM transfers are smoother than others. For example, at the present time (1998) some transfers between computers do not include PAF sources while they do include the notes (such as from PAF 3.0 to Family Tree Maker). The sources are not converted in Family Tree Maker and therefore are lost. The notes are retained.

Some way of recording source citations is a very important part of your genealogical records, and therefore of your genealogy software program.

You need to be able to record, and later retrieve, examine, update, add to, print, and download in automated form your source citations. Genealogical information that has no known source becomes of little value. If you recorded your own information, and you have personal knowledge of those facts, say so! Personal knowledge of one who actually knows the facts is a valid and important source. (But if you are citing personal knowledge as a source for your ancestor born in 1715, then it is not acceptable, because you could not have been a living witness nor have personal knowledge of those events.)

Some software programs give you freedom to record notes as you choose, while others provide more guidelines.

A guideline for determining how much detail to record in your notes could be to answer three basic needs to allow yourself or others to:

- know how to access the source at a later date.
- generally evaluate the information in the source.
- generally determine if the source might be useful for other genealogical purposes.

For example, if you used a U.S. census record, include the year, state, county, and city or township, and, if you know it, the page number. If you used it at a library, including the name of the library and their call number for this source will be helpful.

If the census record was a microfilm of the original record, this may be noted or if it was a transcribed (printed copy), this is helpful to know and to allow evaluation of the source.

If you used a compiled source, you may want to indicate this, but also state that it used cemetery, probate, and family Bible records for the information (but don't list those as your sources unless you personally looked at them or at a copy of them). An excellent reference book with explanations and examples of source citations and evidence notes is *Evidence! Citations & Analysis for the Family Historian*, 1997, by Elizabeth Shown Mills.

Examples of compiled sources include: (1) the McCubbins collection covering records of several counties of North Carolina, available in many genealogical libraries on microfilm (it was compiled by a man named McCubbins); (2) records compiled by the genealogical committees of the Daughters of the American Revolution (DAR). (These are totally different from their lineage application papers.) These collected records include cemetery records, Bible records, probate extracts, family records and often can be used to supplement meager locality records to help trace family migrations and fill in records of children who died along the way, etc.

For example, your family may be in California and you do not know where they came from. You may find a Bible record carefully preserved by the DAR chapter in California, which states that the Bible was originally owned by John Deweese of Greenville, South Carolina. You can begin to search the records of Greenville, South Carolina, and may find land records or a Church reference to John Deweese who later disappears from the records of that area.

Keep in mind that compiled records may contain errors. For example, in copying a family Bible record, the person acting as scribe may have skipped a child's name and copied the birth date of that child for the next child. It is always necessary to use several records and not be alarmed by the lack of complete agreement among them. As you study multiple records about your family, you can usually determine the details that are most likely to be correct.

You may also wish to include notes on evidence that the source provided which you feel is important to your research, such as specific details of how this person or family was listed in the record. For example, "Jane Parker was listed as the wife of Robert Parker and the daughter of John Drake"; or, "a single cemetery stone located in the Horn section of the Old Vassalboro cemetery listed Captain Jeremiah Farwell and his wife Ruth."

If you are going to use a notes field to cite your sources, one way you might organize your sources within the notes area is to label each basic fact, and then record your sources:

```
!BIRTH: certificate in posses-
sion of John Doe, 1960 Ponce
de Leon Ave., Tryon, NC,
address as of April 1992.
- 1860 census (lists Harry as
a child, age 8 months, born
1859, in home of Elijah and
Betsey Nichols), Starks,
Somerset, Maine (FHL film no.
803452, typed page no. 13;
handwritten page no. 153).
- 1905 state census of WI
(Phillips, Price County, FHL
film 1020981, page 172) lists
Harrison as a parent, age 45,
born Maine, both parents born
Maine; occupation: lumber
salesman, owned his home).

!MARRIAGE: Vital Records of
Starks, Somerset, ME (FHL film
000000, page 00) for 1st mar-
riage. International
Genealogical Index (IGI) 1988
edition, for the 2nd marriage
(batch no. A00000). Ancestral
File, 1990 edition for both
marriages.

DEATHS: Family Bible of Harry
H and Mabel Farwell Nichols,
in possession of Veva Nichols
Cramer in 1960; obituary;
tombstone in Ladysmith, WI
```

PAF has a special feature to allow you to determine in advance which source citations you want to automatically print on your family group records and in transferring your automated data (see page 61). This is done by typing an exclamation point (!) directly in front of the first word in the note, as !BIRTH. Everything will be considered part of that note until a blank line separates it from the next item.

This allows you to record biographical and personal information that you may not want to send to others by simply omitting the exclamation point from in front of the note. (You have the option of including all notes when you print or download, or just the "tagged" notes with the exclamation point.)

For example, you may want to record that Harry Nichols was 5 feet 10 inches tall, had black hair, and due to health problems had his leg amputated at the hip about five years before his death. (This would not be part of your sources, and you would not want to have an exclamation point in front of this note.)

Most programs, including PAF, allow you to delete words or lines or blocks of lines from the notes fields, as well as to add words, phrases, or blocks to the notes. Read your instructions for how to do this.

9. Obtain on-line help

   All software programs have some help available to you on the screen.

   – Read the instructions on the screen. They will usually tell you what to do and how to do it. (Try it if you are not sure; you won't hurt the computer.)

   – Most software programs also have "Help" messages that can be displayed to help you with various functions and screens. Many of these access this help by pressing the F1 function key (the key at the top of the keyboard that has F1 as a label). Other programs, such as PAF, have another key or combination of keys to press to display these messages.

- The help message displayed will depend on where you have the cursor at the time you press the help key(s). For example, if you are in the name field, it will display more about how to type names. If you are in a date field, it will display help on how to record dates; if you are in a locality field, it will display help on recording places.

10. Short-cuts

- Reading the instructions on the screen will help you more than almost anything else.

- Some "short-cuts" are regular features, while others are options that you must learn about in order to engage the option.

- It is often possible to ditto words (such as names of people and places and dates) in genealogy. Each software program will have its own method of doing this, if it provides that capability.

- PAF allows you to ditto by using the F8 key, and selecting the information (such as a name of a place) you want to ditto.

- PAF allows you to automatically match/merge records that have the same AFN (Ancestral File number). This is designed to enable you to have the computer merge two records for the same person with the same AFN number (see page 44) in the records downloaded from Ancestral File.

If you download 4 generations of your pedigree chart today, and next week you download generations 5-7, you will have some duplicate records needed to link your pedigree together. You can personally match/merge these records in PAF by using either the manual "automatic" or "merge two records" features, which both allow you to look at each record and decide that you want to merge it.

Note: You should always have a good back-up copy of your data file before you begin making corrections and merges in case something goes wrong. It is always recommended that you keep an up-to-date backup of any computer file, because problems do sometimes develop that ruin your data file, such as an electrical outage, for example. If you have a good back-up, you can replace the ruined file. (If not, tears won't bring it back, but they may help you feel better.)

11. Ability to suppress or engage certain options (Utilities)

Most software programs allow you to make certain choices when you set up (configure) your program. There are "default" settings, sometimes labeled preferences, which are the way your computer will automatically do things. Then there is a way to temporarily (or permanently) change some or all of these settings.

We will discuss a few of these options. You can choose:

- to change to another data file on your hard disk, or to access a database on a floppy diskette in the A or B drives of your computer.

- whether to include RIN (record identification numbers) on your printouts.

- whether to display LDS ordinance dates on screens and reports (see page 27 for more information).

- the number of generations to print on your pedigree charts (4, 5, 6). If you print generations, some of the information will be abbreviated.

- to use letter-size or legal size paper; to use continuous sheet or single sheets for letter size.

- to have the surname print in all capital letters (without typing it in all caps).

12. Share your information

It is possible to share your information with others, or to have others

The Genesis of Your Genealogy

share their information with you, without retyping it. For more information, see pages 24 and 61.

13. Help is available

    – User Groups

    Local users of software often create support groups to help each other. Check your local library or the publisher of your software to locate those in your area.

    – Books

    Read your own user manual that is provided with your genealogy software package.

    There are many others available.

    – Periodicals

    Genealogical Computing (Salt Lake City, UT: Ancestry Inc.)

    NGS/CIG Digest (Arlington, VA: National Genealogical Society, Computer Interest Group)

    – Telephone Support

    Your genealogy software publisher may provide a phone support service.

IV. USING COMPUTERS TO SHARE GENEALOGICAL INFORMATION

It is possible to make a copy of all or selected genealogical records from one computerized database, and share it with others without retyping the information.

A. Two ways to share information without retyping it

- Copy the file

    You can make a copy of an entire data file by following the instructions for you to copy a file from the hard disk or to make a copy of the file from the floppy diskette. This will be the entire database and must be used in the same software program on the same type of computer. Someone else can use the entire database but cannot add the records to an existing database without retyping the information.

- Create a GEDCOM copy of the file

    You can make a copy of all or part of your genealogical data file by using a GEDCOM format, and add it either to a new or an existing data file. GEDCOM stands for Genealogical Data Communications. It converts the records

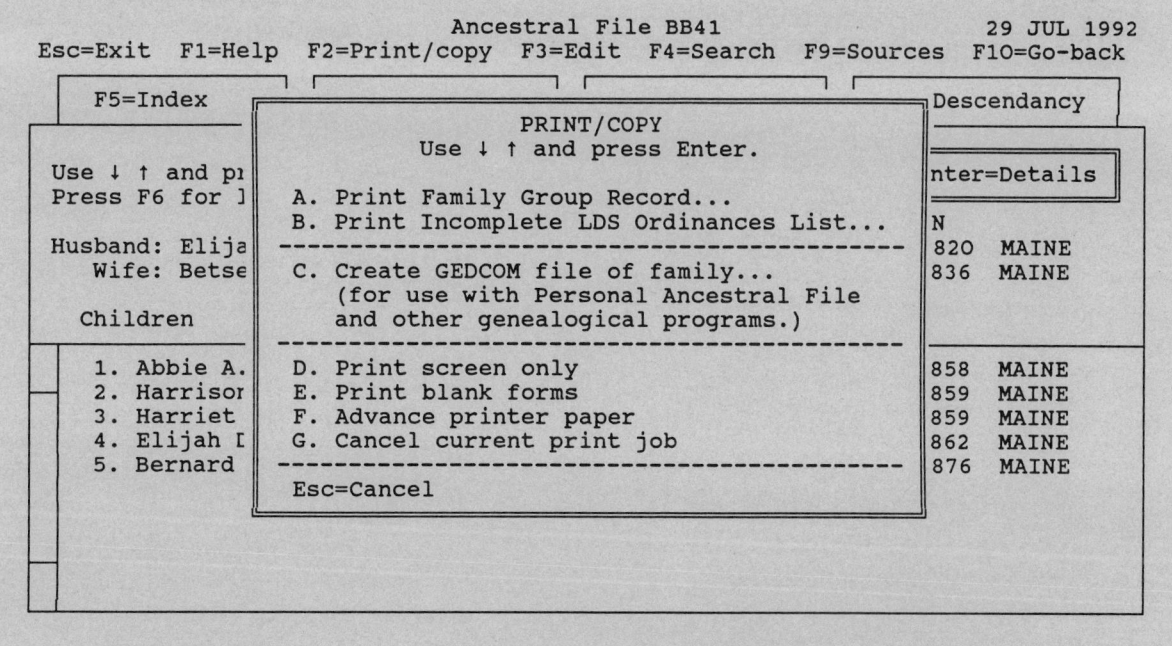

```
                       Ancestral File BB41                    29 JUL 1992
 Esc=Exit   F1=Help   F2=Print/copy   F3=Edit   F4=Search   F9=Sources   F10=Go-back
┌─────────────────┐  ┌──────────────────────────────────────┐  ┌──────────────────┐
│    F5=Index     │  │              PRINT/COPY              │  │   Descendancy    │
├─────────────────┤  │       Use ↓ ↑ and press Enter.       │  ├──────────────────┤
│ Use ↓ ↑ and pr  │  │                                      │  │ nter=Details     │
│ Press F6 for 1  │  │  A. Print Family Group Record...     │  │                  │
│                 │  │  B. Print Incomplete LDS Ordinances List... │ N           │
│ Husband: Elija  │  │  ----------------------------------- │  │ 820   MAINE      │
│    Wife: Betse  │  │  C. Create GEDCOM file of family...  │  │ 836   MAINE      │
│                 │  │     (for use with Personal Ancestral File │                │
│ Children        │  │      and other genealogical programs.)    │                │
│                 │  │  ----------------------------------- │  │                  │
│   1. Abbie A.   │  │  D. Print screen only                │  │ 858   MAINE      │
│   2. Harrison   │  │  E. Print blank forms                │  │ 859   MAINE      │
│   3. Harriet    │  │  F. Advance printer paper            │  │ 859   MAINE      │
│   4. Elijah D   │  │  G. Cancel current print job         │  │ 862   MAINE      │
│   5. Bernard    │  │  ----------------------------------- │  │ 876   MAINE      │
│                 │  │  Esc=Cancel                          │  │                  │
│                 │  └──────────────────────────────────────┘  │                  │
└─────────────────┘                                            └──────────────────┘
```

FIGURE 41 - *Menu from Ancestral File that allows you to copy data to a diskette in GEDCOM* into a format that computers understand but that is rather difficult for people to read. Each line has a label (such as name), with levels (surname, given names), and various computer instructions to tell the computer what to do with the specific information in that line when it again converts it to linked genealogical records in the new data file.

GEDCOM (1) does not require that you include the entire file, (2) allows you to add the records to a file that already has records in it, and (3) does not require that the same software be used when you "upload" it into a new data file. The process of making a GEDCOM copy is called "downloading" (or copying) or exporting records; the process of adding the records to either a new data file or to an already existing one is called "uploading" or importing the records.

However, the genealogy software in both the system from which you are downloading and the system to which you are uploading records must be able to handle records in GEDCOM format.

B. Many genealogy software programs support GEDCOM

- All FamilySearch data files (except the Family History Library Catalog) handle GEDCOM files. You can download information from them and take it home to add to your personal data files. There is no charge to do this, but you must provide the diskette.

- You can add your records to Ancestral File by downloading them in a GEDCOM format and submitting them to Ancestral File in Salt Lake City, Utah. Again, there is no charge to do this. And you retain the right to use your records in whatever other way you may choose.

- The Personal Ancestral File (PAF) handles three types of GEDCOM files tailored for different needs. One of these files is made especially to help you submit your family research to Ancestral File.

Each option will walk you through the process by displaying instructions on the screen.

To either share your information with a friend (whose computer has GEDCOM ability), to create a GEDCOM file to move part of your records from one data file to another on your own computer, or to upload records received from another file (in GEDCOM format) into one of your data files, choose the first option.

To submit your information to Ancestral File, choose the second option.

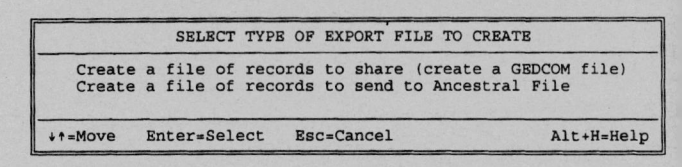

```
┌─────────────────────────────────────────────────────────┐
│           SELECT TYPE OF EXPORT FILE TO CREATE          │
├─────────────────────────────────────────────────────────┤
│  Create a file of records to share (create a GEDCOM file)│
│  Create a file of records to send to Ancestral File     │
├─────────────────────────────────────────────────────────┤
│  ↓↑=Move    Enter=Select    Esc=Cancel      Alt+H=Help  │
└─────────────────────────────────────────────────────────┘
```

FIGURE 42 - PAF Export menu (creates GEDCOM files)

To submit your information for LDS temple ordinances, choose the third option (this option will not appear unless you have selected to show LDS detail in your preferences for this data file). If you wish to have it appear, go into Preferences, and on the second item choose Y for yes. (See figure 22.)

Options 2 and 3 assist you in preparing your records to submit to these files. For example, option 2 checks each record and provides comments on those that need more information, etc.

- A guide titled *FamilySearch : Contributing Information to Ancestral File* lists four steps in contributing your information to Ancestral File:

  1. Prepare your information.
  2. Enter your information into a computer file.
  3. Create a GEDCOM file on diskette.
  4. Send your diskette to Ancestral File.

  This guide is available free of charge from the Family History Library, 35 North West Temple Street, Salt Lake City, UT 84150 or from Family History Centers.

- Detailed instructions, including illustrations for using PAF to submit names to Ancestral File are found in the publication *Genealogy in the Computer Age: Understanding FamilySearch , vol. 1 (Ancestral File , International Genealogical Index , Social Security Death Index), revised edition* by Elizabeth L. Nichols (Salt Lake City, UT: Family History Educators).

PART THREE: GLOSSARY OF TERMS FOR THE GENEALOGIST/FAMILY HISTORIAN

The following list not only defines but also often explains the terms given.

Abstract

This word has two totally different meanings, both useful to the family historian: (1) a summary that gives the essential facts but does not quote the source word for word; (2) not easy to understand, or general.

Ancestor

Someone from whom you are descended — a parent, grandparent, great-grandparent, etc. Ancestors' names appear on one's pedigree chart.

Ancestral File

A pedigree-linked file of information submitted to the LDS Church since 1978 for sharing, limited mostly to records of persons who are now deceased. Records can be displayed, printed on paper, or downloaded in automated form. Displays include pedigree charts or family groups, as well as individual records and names and addresses of those who submitted the information. It is a part of FamilySearch, and is on compact disc. The 1996 edition contains over 29 million records. (1996 edition refers to the date the information was taken from the master file to create the compact disc, and may not be the same as the date of distribution.) Future editions will include millions more. The computer merges records that match, and thus eliminates most duplication; it does occasionally make errors. Please verify the information found in Ancestral File. But it is a wonderful place to begin.

Everyone is invited to help build the file by submitting records on your ancestry. If possible, first consult the file to see if some or all of your ancestors' records have already been submitted. Submissions of automated data in GEDCOM format should be mailed to: Ancestral File, Family History Department, 50 East North Temple Street, Salt Lake City, Utah 84150. (See page 44.)

Accredited Genealogist (A.G.) *See* Genealogist.

Approximate *See* Dates and places.

Artifact

A cultural specimen or object used to communicate a message. For example, a dish that has been in the family for more than one generation, or a tool used in the 1800s are artifacts.

Backup

A copy of your computer file that serves as a security copy, in case the data in your regular data file should become damaged.

CD-ROM

A compact disc that can be read by using an addition on a personal computer called a CD-ROM drive. Data cannot usually be changed. It is similar to a music disc for your CD player. (There are also compact discs now that allow you to read and/or write to them.)

Blended families

A family unit that includes natural children, stepchildren, foster children, half-brothers and half–sisters, and adopted children, all as part of a single family group.

Boundary changes *See* places.

Calendar of Events

An outline of the major events of a person's life, telling **when, what,** and **where** arranged in chronological sequence. The calendar of events can be used to determine when and where your family were when specific events occurred (such as births, marriages, deaths, census taking) to locate any records about members of the family. It can also be used to determine where to fit in specific incidents in a written family history. (See page 17.)

Cemetery records

Records created about burials. They consist of two types: sexton records (office records) and tombstones, both of which can provide valuable genealogical information.

Census records

Records that were created to number the population, especially sponsored by governments to determine the available men for soldiers. The amount of information given in a census varies, according to the needs and purposes of those who sponsored the census. Early census records usually listed only the head of the household by name (if that much), and often listed the number of males and females within each age group (such as 2 males ages 5-10 years, 1 male over 45, 1 female over 45).

Beginning after 1840, census records started to include information on every member of the family, and often gave details on each, such as the name, sex, age, state or country of birth, and sometimes the place of birth for the father and mother of each person listed, etc. Beginning in 1880, U.S. censuses also included the relationship of each person to the head of the household.

Rights of privacy of living persons make recent censuses confidential. The 1920 U.S. census is the latest one to become available for public searching in this country.

The federal census was usually taken every ten years, and sometimes local areas (such as states) took a census in between (for example, the U.S. census was taken in 1900 and 1910; the Wisconsin state census was taken in 1905).

Use indexes! Many census records have been indexed. Usually these are for an entire state, county, or region. These indexes may be available in book form, on microfiche, or for searches by computer. They usually give only the name of the head of household with the page reference within the state, county, and town; or the names of each member of a household with limited information and reference to the census entry which provides greater detail. (While these are very helpful, they are almost never complete, and some names have been misread and so are filed incorrectly.) If you don't find the name of your ancestor in an index and you are sure the family was living in this area at that time, it may be worth the effort to go directly to the census and look for the family.

Soundex indexes. For U.S. censuses, beginning in 1880 many indexes use what is known as a Soundex system. This means that surnames that sound alike are grouped together. These require using a "soundex code" to find the surname, and then the entries are arranged alphabetically by given name within that surname code. The first letter of the surname is used, and then each consonant is given a numeric value (for 3 letters), while each vowel is dropped along with other similar-sounding letters (a, e, i, o, u, y, w, h).

The soundex key is:

1	b, p, f, v
2	c, s, k, g, j, x, z, q
3	d, t
4	m, n
6	r

For example, if the name is NICHOLS, begin with N and then drop the I, code the C, drop the H and the O, code the L and the S. You have N-242. If you have double letters or two letters with the same code, drop one of them, as Morrow would be coded M-600.

(See figure 14 for an example of a census record.)

Certified Genealogist (C.G.) *See* Genealogist

Christening

Baptism into most churches. It often occurred a few hours or days following the birth of a child, and often was recorded for places and time periods when there are no birth records. For this reason, christening records are a major source for family history information. They may be listed in library catalogs under church records or under vital records, and are often referred to as parish registers. (Note: LDS blessing dates of infants are not christening dates; LDS baptism does not occur until a person reaches the age of eight years or more.)

Church of Jesus Christ of Latter-day Saints, The

A church whose doctrines and beliefs center in Jesus Christ as Savior and Redeemer and includes the belief that families can be together after death, if certain Church ordinances are performed by proper priesthood authority. (The final judgment of a person's worthiness is between that person and the Lord; and individuals can choose to accept or reject the work done in their behalf.) The Church encourages its members to trace their genealogies and provides access to records to assist them. The Church graciously shares its genealogical resources with others who wish to trace genealogies. (Also known as the Mormon Church; the LDS Church;

and by names of organizations within the Church such as the Family History Department and the Family History Library; or its affiliate organization, the Genealogical Society of Utah).

Collateral

Belonging to the same family lines but not in a direct descent, such as a cousin in any degree.

Compact disc

A disc similar to a small record, used for storage of large amounts of automated data. It can be used in personal computers with a CD-ROM drive.

Computer hardware

The computer base (where the drives are located), monitor (terminal, screen) where the information is displayed, the printer, etc. Computers cannot do anything until they have software loaded into them. (*See also* Computer software.)

Computer software

Programs that have been written to tell the computer how to do specific things, such as a "word processor" that allows you to type information into the computer and have it displayed on a computer screen, edit (change) it, print it, save it, retrieve it, etc.; or to type information and link names with associated event dates and places into pedigrees and family groups. Software is loaded into the computer's "memory" (storage space in the hardware) when you want to use that program to tell the computer what to do. The software may be stored on the computer's hard disk or on a floppy diskette that is inserted in the computer drive each time it is to be used. (*See also* Computer hardware.)

Concrete

Specific, not general. In writing, we should seek to be concrete in our descriptions of people and events.

Culture

"The concepts, habits, skills, art, instruments, institutions, etc., of a given people in a given period; civilization."

Dates

The day, month, and year of an event, or any part of it (such as the year only, or the month only). In genealogy, dates are written: day, month, year, as 2 July 1992. Always write out all four digits of the year, and use the letter abbreviations for the month to avoid confusion.

Dates may be complete (containing day, month, and year), or incomplete (lacking one or more of these elements). They may be exact, calculated, approximated, or estimated (see below).

"About" dates are dates that are unknown, but estimated often from other family members' events, such as the birth of a brother or sister or child. These dates are preceded by the word about, or the abbreviation "abt," or "Ca" for the Latin term Circa, meaning about.

Approximated dates are "about" dates. (See above.)

"Calculated" dates are derived from an age at a stated date, such as "died 1901, age 79 years" (which would make the person born 1822).

Some people do use the term "about" in front of calculated dates, because they may not be exact, but it is usually better to write the year followed by the basis, if there is space, such as "born 1822 (age 79 in 1901)."

"Exact" dates are the complete date of the actual event, such as a birth occurred on 26 May 1937.

"Or" dates are when you know that an event occurred on one of two dates, such as 4 July or 5 June; or, 1787 or 1789.

"Double dating" is used to show two different calendars for the same event. This is used in older genealogical records, because for a time both the Julian and the Gregorian calendars were in use in different parts of the world and one began the year in January while the other began the year in March. So from January through March 25, you might see 4 Feb 1738/39 (meaning if the year began in January it was 1739; if it began in March it was 1738). For more information, see *Genealogy in the Computer Age: Understanding FamilySearch* by Elizabeth L. Nichols, volume 2.

Daughters of the American Revolution (DAR)

An organization of women who can prove descent from someone who gave service to the cause of liberty during the Revolutionary War period. Its objectives are: (1) to perpetuate the memory and spirit of the men and women who achieved American Independence; (2) to carry out the injunction of George Washington in his farewell address to the American people "to promote, as an object of primary importance, institutions for the general diffusion of knowledge," thus developing an enlightened public opinion, and affording to young and old such advantages as shall develop in them the largest capacity for performing the duties of American Citizens; (3) to cherish, maintain, and extend the institutions of American freedom, to foster true patriotism and love of country, and to aid in securing for mankind all the blessings of liberty. Among the services for which DAR is known are preserving records of genealogical significance, encouraging and supporting the teaching of American history in the public schools, and assisting the foreign born who are in process of becoming American Citizens. The national organization, located at 1776 D Street NW, Washington, D.C. 20006, directs the organization within each state, and each state has as many local units (chapters) as there is need for.

Deeds

Land records. In the earlier time periods deeds are an important genealogical source, because they often state or imply relationship. Land often passed from one generation of a family to another. Neighbors and witnesses were often relatives or others who had come from the same original places. In using deeds, there are indexes arranged by the names of the buyer (grantee) and for the seller (grantor). These indexes refer to the date, book number, and page number of the actual deed, which is usually located in the county courthouse, though microfilm copies are often available in genealogical libraries or archives.

Demography

The study of events that normally take place in a family setting or in the formation of a family, such as births, marriages, deaths, and migrations; or "the science of vital statistics."

Descendant

Someone who is a child, grandchild, great-grandchild (in any generation of descent); moving downward from an ancestor.

Directory

A space within the computer where certain files are stored. (*See also* Path.)

Direct-line family

Ancestors whose names appear on your pedigree chart and all of their children.

Discrepancies

Differences. In family history/genealogy, you will often find small differences, such as the birth date of a person being recorded 31 March 1746 in this record, and 20 Dec 1747 in another record (yet they appear to be describing the same person); or that Uncle Harry moved to Indiana in 1844, when another family record says it was 1834. Don't be upset by these differences; record them all, and see if you can find original or primary records to verify one or the other; if not, record both with the word or between the dates. See page 18.

Diskette

A small disk, either 5¼ inches or 3½ inches in size for storing computerized data. The diskette can be used in personal computers, or to download information from FamilySearch in GEDCOM format which you can take home and use in a personal computer (with the right software program). Also referred to as a floppy disk.

There are low density and high density diskettes, which refers to the amount of data the diskette can hold. There are double-sided designations for each double density (DS DD) refers to the low density ones, while double sided high density (DS HD) does not. Older computers can handle only low density (DS DD) ones, while newer computers can usually handle both. (Computers can, of course, be upgraded from floppy diskettes to a hard disk, or from low density only to also handle high density diskettes.)

Document

This word has two different meanings: (Noun) "Anything printed, written, etc., relied upon to record or prove something"; (verb) "to provide references as proof or support."

Download

The process of copying automated records from one computer data file, using a genealogical communications format called GEDCOM, so the records can be added to another computer file without having to retype the information. The information in the first file is not changed. This is also called Exporting.

Emigrate

To leave one's place of residence and move elsewhere, such as to move from one country to another. Emigration records help trace family migrations.

Empathy

"The projection of one's own personality into the personality of another in order to understand him better." For the family historian, this includes understanding the background of the person and realizing he would react differently than you, but understanding how it would make him/her feel.

Environment

"All the conditions, circumstances, and influences surrounding and affecting the development of." The environment of the 1800s in rural America was different from our environment today. We need to consider the way things were when the events occurred.

Evaluate

Determine the significance of something. In genealogical research, it means to study the facts individually and together to see if they fit and, where there are discrepancies, to determine, based on evidence and facts, which one is most probably correct. Careful evaluation of information can keep you from tracing the wrong ancestral family, thinking they are yours when they are not.

Evidence

Something that provides proof, or clues, that help determine facts. Indication; inference.

Direct evidence tells you facts, as stated in the records. Indirect evidence tells you something that is not stated in the records. For example, if a child is born in Onondaga County, NY, there is direct evidence that the family had some association with this place. If the census records list only one John Harvey in the county, and you find a land record or a church record referring to John Harvey, this is indirect evidence that the land record or church would refer to your particular John Harvey; if the census shows there are three men by that name in the county, you need more information (facts or evidence) before you can determine if the land record refers to your ancestor or to another man by that name. Evidence must be considered in relation to all known facts and other evidence.

Ethnic

A member of a minority or nationality group that is part of a larger community, such as a Japanese settlement in the United States; a Polish settlement, an Irish settlement, etc., which is distinguished by customs, characteristics, languages, etc., different from the larger community.

Export

A term used in Personal Ancestral File to refer to copying or downloading GEDCOM records to share with others. (*See also* Import.)

Extant

Still in existence.

Extracted

An LDS Church term for entries that were extracted (copied) primarily from original (microfilmed) records of birth, christening, or marriage, where selected pertinent genealogical information was "extracted" from the larger amount of information, and automated. *See also* Extraction Programs.

The *Parish and Vital Records List* (on microfiche) describes the records, localities, and time periods covered, and may indicate whether or not the extracted records are in the current edition of the International Genealogical Index.

Extraction Programs

Programs of The Church of Jesus Christ of Latter-day Saints in which volunteers are assigned to extract pertinent genealogical information from selected records for selected time periods. For many years, there was only one "Extraction Program" (also known as the Stake Extraction Program or the Controlled Extraction Program). This program limited the selection of records to those of birth, christening, or marriage. However, the Family Records Extraction program is being merged with the Stake Extraction program, and this will include a greater variety of record types. This distinction becomes important as one evaluates the records extracted in these programs. The source of an entry in the IGI can be identified by the batch number and/or film number associated with the entry. (*See also* Extracted.)

Family

The basic unit of society in all civilizations. A family may refer to a single unit, usually consisting of a father, mother, and at least one child; an extended family may include grandparents, aunts, uncles, cousins, etc. Nontypical families may include only one parent and one or more children.

Family group record form

A form showing one father, mother, and all their children, including names, dates, and places of vital events in their lives.

Family historian

A writer or compiler of family history; an authority or a specialist in family history.

Family history

The study of the history of families, with emphasis on both genealogical detail (names, dates, places, relationships) and the stories and attitudes that make people individuals, and that are passed on in the form of heritage. The history of a family gives equal emphasis to each member of that family (*see also* Personal history, and Genealogy).

Family History Center™ (FHC)

Branches of the Family History Library in Salt Lake City, Utah. Formerly known as branch genealogical libraries, these are often small centers, usually located in LDS meetinghouses throughout the world, where volunteers are available to assist those who wish to use the facilities for family research. They are often open only limited hours. Their collections usually include FamilySearch (the Family History Library Catalog, the Ancestral File, the International Genealogical Index [IGI], the Personal Ancestral File genealogy software, and other computer programs and files), plus the Family History Library Catalog, and 1992 edition of the IGI on microfiche; and may also include books, microfiche and microfilms of various records. In addition, the records listed in the Library catalog that are available in microform (microfilm or microfiche) can be ordered and used at the Family History Center for a small loan fee. These centers may be listed in the phone book under The Church of Jesus Christ of Latter-day Saints, or a list of those near you can be obtained free of charge by writing to the Family History Library, 35 North West Temple Street, Salt Lake City, UT 84150, or from the Internet at www.lds.org.

Family History Department

The name of a specific department that is responsible for genealogical activities within The Church of Jesus Christ of Latter-day Saints (Mormons).

Family History Library™ (FHL)

The Family History Library of The Church of Jesus Christ of Latter-day Saints (Mormons, LDS, Genealogical Society of Utah), located in Salt Lake City, Utah, at 35 North West Temple Street (downtown and easily accessible). It is the largest genealogical library in the world. Its vast resources are open to the public without charge, and most of its collection can be ordered and used at its 3,000 Family History Centers throughout the world.

Family History Library Catalog™ (FHLC)

The catalog that describes the vast genealogical collection of the Family History Library in Salt Lake City, Utah. It has two media of access — on microfiche and on compact disc as part of FamilySearch.

The catalog provides for several different approaches to finding records, including a unique locality search, as well as searches by surname (family name), author, title, and subject. Copies of the FHLC are available at Family History Centers throughout the world, and at many other major libraries. (*See also* Family History Library and Family History Center.) For detailed guidelines in using the Catalog and understanding the information provided in the catalog entry, see *Genealogy in the Computer Age: Understanding FamilySearch®*, volume 2, by Elizabeth L. Nichols.

FamilySearch®

A series of computer programs and data files created by The Church of Jesus Christ of Latter-day Saints, to be run on a personal computer with a CD-ROM drive. The files, available on compact disc, include the International Genealogical Index, Ancestral File, the Family History Library Catalog, U.S. Social Security Death Index 1962-96, Military Index (U.S. citizens who died in Vietnam and Korea), with others soon to follow. No modem access presently exists. FamilySearch is presently available only at LDS Family History Centers and the main Family History Library in Salt Lake City

...d in some other libraries. It is not presently ...ailable for purchase by individuals.

...che

...shortened form of the word *microfiche.*

...lm

...shortened form of the word *microfilm.*

...lio

...ftware that allows full-text searching of a file on ...computer; that is, it allows you to type in a word ... words and the computer will quickly tell you ...w many times that word or combination of ...ords appear in the document; Folio then allows ...u to go to each occurrence of the term. For ...ample, if you are looking for Mary Woodcock, it ...ould tell you how many occurrences of the word *...ary* and how many occurrences of the word *...oodcock* appear in the document, and how many ...mes they appear on the same page. This would ...t mean that the name Mary Woodcock would ...pear on every page reference, but it could be ...ary Wilson in one place and Encore Woodcock in ...other sentence on that page. Folio is the back...ound program used in the SourceGuide now ...vailable from the LDS Church, which you can ...urchase and use on your own computer at home.

...lklore

...aditions, beliefs, and customs that are handed ...wn from generation to generation, often by ...ord of mouth or songs.

...eedom of Information Act

... United States law that makes certain types of ...deral information available to the public. The ...ocial Security Death Index is an example of a file ...ade available under this Act.

...unction keys

... set of keys on the computer keyboard with an F ... front of the number. By pressing the key a cer...in function will be activated; for example, F4 ...ay display the request screen, and F12 may begin ... search, or F1 may display help messages.

...azetteer

... reference book that lists places, with their ...escriptions, including jurisdictions in which they ...eside, and often historical facts such as when they ...ere created and name changes that have occurred.

Example from a gazetteer, *The Length and Breadth of Maine:* "Vassalborough. Town. Kennebec county. Bounds, WINSLOW, CHINA, AUGUSTA, SIDNEY. Area in acres: Land 28,640, inland water 1440, bog or swamps 422, total 30,080. Settled 1760. Incorporated Apr 26, 1771, the 22nd town. Part set off to form SIDNEY Jan 30, 1792. Part of CHINA annexed Feb 18, 1829. Principal settlements, Vassalborough, East Vassalborough, North Vassalborough."

GEDCOM

An abbreviation for *Genealogical Data Communications.* It formats the data (names, dates, places, relationships [linkages], sources) into a form that can be transferred from one computer system to another without having to rekey the information.

The Family History Library in Salt Lake City maintains a list of "registered" genealogy software programs for personal computers that provide the ability to handle GEDCOM files that can communicate with FamilySearch files (such as Ancestral File).

Genealogical Society of Utah (GSU)

An organization that specializes in microfilming records throughout the world to preserve the genealogies of mankind by preserving the records of births, marriages, and deaths with some related sources for all countries and time periods of the past. Presently it has over 200 cameras filming records in 40 countries. Negative copies of the film are stored in a records vault specially built to preserve microfilms, and a positive copy is made available for use by researchers at the main Family History Library in Salt Lake City or its Family History Centers throughout the world. It also cooperates with other organizations to preserve, share, and organize records and the data contained in those records. For example, projects of this type include the indexing of the Civil War records of the United States, which is a joint undertaking between the GSU, the National Park Service, the National Archives, and the Federation of Genealogical Societies; and the indexing of the 1881 British census, which was a joint undertaking of the GSU and the Federation of Family History Societies in Great Britain. The resulting data files will eventually be made available as part of FamilySearch. GSU is an affiliate of The Church of Jesus Christ of Latter-day Saints (Mormons).

Genealogist, Accredited (A.G.)

Someone who has passed written and verbal examinations to test the knowledge and skills as a genealogical researcher and compiler of pedigrees and family histories, after hours of experience in this field. The program is a service provided by The Church of Jesus Christ of Latter-day Saints (Genealogical Society of Utah), but the accredited genealogists as such are not employees of the Church. Their skills have been tested, and they agree to adhere to ethical conduct in their dealings with their clients. If they wish to take clients their names are included on the list of accredited genealogists for a specific geographical area. Such a list may be obtained upon request from:

Family History Library
35 North West Temple Street
Salt Lake City, UT 84150

Genealogist, Certified (C.G.)

There are several categories of specialists certified by the Board for Certification of Genealogists, including:

Certified Genealogical Record Searcher (C.G.R.S.), who is certified to search original and published records, and has an understanding of all sources of a genealogical nature for an area, but is not certified to construct a pedigree or prepare a family history.

Certified Genealogist (C.G.), who not only conducts research among primary sources and studies secondary works but also works to solve genealogical problems and constructs genealogies of families based upon investigation of the sources and careful analysis of the evidence.

Certified American Lineage Specialist (C.A.L.S), who is certified to prepare a single line of descent and is competent to determine the authenticity of evidence and acceptability of original and compiled source materials.

Other specialists include Certified American Indian Lineage Specialist (C.A.I.L.S.), Certified Genealogical Lecturer (C.G.L., which must include at least a C.G.R.S. certification), and a Certified Genealogical Instructor (C.G.I), which must include being a certified genealogist. Lists of these certified specialists are available from the Board of Certification, P. O. Box 19165, Washington, D.C. 20036-0165.

Genealogy

The study of one's ancestry, with emphasis on names, dates, places, and relationships.

Genealogy in the Computer Age: Understanding FamilySearch®, **volumes 1 and 2.**

Publication by Elizabeth L. Nichols that describes the programs and files of FamilySearch; vol. 1: 56 pages, 66 illustrations, includes Ancestral File, the IGI, and the Social Security Death Index; vol. 2: 8 pages, 86 illustrations; includes PAF 3.0, the Family History Library Catalog, more resource files, how to use all these files in harmony, case studies, and guidelines.

Genealogical resource files

Large computer files that contain genealogical information which can be accessed as part of FamilySearch (such as Ancestral File and International Genealogical Index [IGI]). *See also* FamilySearch.

Given-name searches

Searches which are based on a person's given name rather than the surname. This applies particularly to those countries (such as Denmark and Sweden) for time periods that used the patronymic naming system (*see* Patronymic).

Grantee

One who is buying land.

Grantor

One who is selling land.

Guideline, Basic

Begin with what you know, and work backward from the known to the unknown.

When you cannot go backward (for example, you cannot find the parents of an ancestor), then come forward one generation (or sometimes even two) and find all the information you can on the children of that person. Clues in the records of the children may help you know where to go or what to look for to discover the next generation back.

Heirloom

"Any valuable or interesting piece of personal property which has belonged to a family for more than one generation; a family relic."

Help

In most computer programs, in addition to the instructions which appear on the screen, help messages have been provided for each field on most screens. Many programs allow you to access this help by pressing the F1 key while the highlight bar is on that field; the explanation will then appear on the screen.

History

"An account of what has happened. An inquiry into thoughts and actions of people in the past; something important enough to be recorded."

Holding file

A feature in some FamilySearch files (such as the International Genealogical Index and Social Security Death Index) that allows you to place multiple records in temporary storage and either print them or download them to a diskette as a group.

Immigrant

A person who comes to another country to take up permanent residence. Immigration records help trace family (or individual) moves.

Import

The process of adding records or images into a computer program or document, such as adding GEDCOM records into your genealogy software program or scanned pictures (images) into a word processing document.

IGI

See International Genealogical Index.

IGI batch number

A reference number in the International Genealogical Index that indicates the source of that entry.

The IGI on compact disc also displays a brief explanation of the source when you press ENTER, and provides additional detail when you press the "Help" key; the microfiche version lists it in a column titled "source." Some batch numbers indicate "extraction" (vital records: C, J, K, M [most M's], and P) while others are forms submitted from compiled records or personal knowledge of relatives. The accuracy of the information varies among entries, but generally the Controlled Extraction entries are good. There are about 100 million Extraction entries in the IGI.

IGI Batch Number Index

A list of all IGI batch numbers with their library call numbers, published on microfiche. It is used to find the sources of information for entries in the International Genealogical Index. (*Note:* The IGI on compact disc includes the film number, and does not require the use of this index.)

International Genealogical Index® (IGI)

An index to millions of names of deceased persons from nearly a hundred countries, originally produced primarily to assist members of The Church of Jesus Christ of Latter-day Saints, but through popular demand made now into a research tool for anyone to use. (Members of the LDS Church now use the Ordinance Index for Church needs; everyone can use the IGI for research.)

This massive index serves as an index to millions of vital events (births, christenings, marriages) — about 100 million entries are from the extraction of vital events, and many compiled records which genealogists everywhere can use to help them in their research, regardless of the purpose of that research.

The Church makes it widely available for use by researchers everywhere.

The IGI was originally published on microfiche, but this has not been updated since the 1992 edition and is limited in what it contains to about 187 million names (versus 284 million on compact disc). Individuals can purchase microfiche in small geographical sections, if desired. The IGI is also available for use on compact disc (CD-ROM) as part of FamilySearch (see page 44). IGI on compact disc cannot presently be purchased by individuals (May 1998). The 1993 edition contains about 200 million names; the 1997 release of the Addendum is a separate set of CD ROMs that contain an additional 84 million names, although some of the same names are found on both the main IGI and the Addendum. The accuracy of information in the IGI varies, and each entry should be evaluated based on its individual source, which is listed in the compact disc version or the key to it is contained in the first letters or numbers of the IGI source batch number or film number. (For example, extraction entries begin with C, J, K, most M, and P.) See also pages 44, 45, and 68.

Jurisdiction

The territory in which an authority may be exercised, as a state has jurisdiction over its citizens; or a county, or a church, etc.

LDS

An abbreviation for The Church of Jesus Christ of Latter-day Saints (Mormons).

Library catalog

A listing and description of all of the records in the collection of a library. (*See also* Family History Library Catalog.)

Maps

An important tool in genealogical research. A map of the area where your ancestors lived showing boundaries, waterways, and mountains at the time they lived there is very helpful.

Menu

In a computer software program, a list of options from which to choose. Usually, pressing ENTER while the highlight bar is on the desired item (or pressing the alphabetical letter beside the option) will tell the computer what you want it to do.

Microfiche

A sheet of microfilm, similar in size to a large card, that can be placed in a special reader and read. Also referred to as fiche. (*See also* Microfilm.)

Microfilm

A roll of film that contains tiny photographs that can be put on a special reading machine and read. Many original records, such as birth records of the 1800s or federal and state census records, may be available on microfilm in libraries. Also referred to as film. (*See also* Microfiche.)

Microfilm item number

The same roll of microfilm may contain many different records, such as family histories (books that were filmed), county histories, biographies, wills. The items are separated by a "title board" that tells the number of this title on the film. Cataloging entries may say "item 10," or "IT 10." This means there will be nine other documents (such as books) on the roll of film before you get to the item you want. There is often no correlation between the items. For example, one may be a gazetteer of Maine, while the next item may refer to church records of Virginia.

Microfilm number

Usually the Family History Library call number for a roll of microfilm. Library catalogs or genealogical data bases (such as Ancestral File or IGI) may refer to them as film numbers, film call numbers, or input sources. Each title found on that roll of film would have the same library call number.

Migration

To move from one place to another, especially from one country to another. Migrations within a country are equally important to the family historian.

MRIN

In Personal Ancestral File (PAF) a marriage record identification number, or family number.

Military Index

An index of United States citizens who died or were reported dead in Vietnam and Korea during military service. The information comes from the U.S. government, and is made available through the Freedom of Information Act. The LDS Church purchased the tapes and make these records available to the public as part of FamilySearch.

Museum

An educational institution that specializes in preserving and exhibiting rare, interesting, or typical artifacts that show the culture(s) of the past.

Names

The words used to identify a person or a place.

People have given names (first and middle—also called Christian names), and surnames (last or family names). A woman usually also has a maiden surname (the name under which she was born and uses until she marries, when she traditionally takes her husband's surname which is passed on to her children). Her name may be written Mabel (Farwell) Nichols. The name is parenthesis is her maiden surname.

Spelling of names often vary from one record to another, but still refer to the same person or family. Do not miss records on your family because the spelling of the name is slightly different (for example, Nickles instead of Nichols).

In earlier years many people were unable to read and write and others were not particular about how their names were spelled. The person making the records (such as the county clerk) would spell the name as he heard it. If he had an English-speaking background and the person speaking had a German-speaking background, for example, the name could have been spelled very differently from the way you would expect to find it. (Watch especially for first letter differences for some names, such as Kramer or Cramer.)

Places have names of different jurisdictions (levels of government) such as towns, counties, states, provinces, or countries; churches have their ecclesiastical divisions. The boundaries may change from time to time. For example, Lumberton, Mississippi was in Pearl River County for many years. Then Lamar County was created in 1904, and Lumberton is now in Lamar County. This may be recorded as Lumberton, Pearl River (now Lamar) MS.

Names of both persons and places may change, and records may be created that identify them by any name by which they were ever known.

When a person is known by more than one name it is usually called an alias as John White, alias Johannes Blanche.

Name-only

The name of a person, with no associated genealogical details.

Network

Computers linked together so they can communicate, using the same databases and software.

Objectivity

The ability to use facts without distortion or personal feelings or prejudices.

Oral history

That which is communicated only by speaking.

Ordinance

A term that refers to religious rites performed by the Church of Jesus Christ of Latter-day Saints. These may be performed during the lifetime of the person or by proxy after death.) The four basic ordinances that are recorded on family group records are: LDS baptism, temple endowment, sealing to parents, and sealing of husband and wife (spouse). Except for baptisms for the living, these ordinances must be performed in an LDS temple.

Ordinance Index

An index used by members of The Church of Jesus Christ of Latter-day Saints for church ordinance dates for deceased persons. The names and genealogical detail are the same as in the International Genealogical Index.

Original records

The actual record made, or a photographic copy of it (such as a microfilm copy). *See also* Transcribed records.

PAF

See Personal Ancestral File

Paleography

The reading of old-style handwriting, such as that used in the 1700s.

Parent Index

An arrangement of records in the International Genealogical Index on compact disc listing the parent(s) names in alphabetical order, followed by the names of the children listed in chronological order of birth or christening. This may bring together records of brothers and sisters. (If the names are common, such as John Smith and Mary, it will also bring together many that are not brothers and sisters, but whose parents have the same names.)

Parish

A record-keeping jurisdiction within a church denomination, presided over by one pastor. (Also in the state of Louisiana, USA, civil divisions similar to counties in other states.)

The area covered by a church parish varies according to local practices. For example, in the British areas, usually each little town had its own parish (church); but in the German areas, a parish often consisted of many little communities (and you must determine to which parish a community belonged in order to find the church records for that area). In the Scandinavian countries (Denmark, for example), the parish register may refer to family by name and the community in which they live, which may be the only way to tell which Jens Larson the record is referring to. In many countries there was a state church, that recorded most of the citizens of the area. But "nonconformist" churches (those that did not conform to the state church) may have existed where records of your ancestors may be found.

In the United States, usually each area had its own church. The early church records may be compiled with the town vital records, or they may be separate, with each denomination having separate records. You must determine which denomination your ancestral family affiliated with in order to find them in the church records. (Sometimes they changed denominations perhaps for doctrinal differences, or because there was no church of their choice in a community.) Sometimes there was no parish or church, but an itinerant minister traveled among many early settlements, and the records he kept may be found anywhere particularly in a historical society or other genealogical collection.

Parish register

Records created by a church to record christenings (baptisms), marriages, and deaths or burials.

Path

In computers, the description that tells the computer where to find a specific file. In most cases, you as the user don't need to know the path, but sometimes to access or print a file, you do need to know its path. For example, whether a file is stored on the hard disk or a floppy disk is part of the path to that file. In Personal Ancestral File, a file may be stored on the hard drive C, within a subdirectory named paf3, in a directory named data, and a subdirectory named Harvie, which would be written: C:\paf3\data\harvie.

Patronymic

A naming custom where the surname (last name) changes every generation, based on the given name of the father. For example, Jens Nielsen is the son of Niels, and his children will be named Jensen (sons of Jens). The term Datter is often used for girls, as, Catherine Jensdatter. (The Scandinavian spelling of Datter [Jensdatter] is commonly used, not the American spelling of Daughter [Jensdaughter].)

Pedigree

Ancestors parents, grandparents, great-grandparents, etc.

Pedigree chart

A chart displaying a person's ancestors, providing an organized arrangement to show the person and his or her two parents, four grandparents, eight great-grandparents, etc., with the relationship of each person and generation to the person whose pedigree is being displayed.

Personal Ancestral File® (PAF)

A computer software program to be used on a personal computer, allowing you to type in names, dates, and places and link them into families for pedigrees, family groups, and other reports. It also has the ability to exchange information via Genealogical Data Communications (GEDCOM) enabling you to import and export (download and upload or copy) data from and to other files and programs without rekeying the information.

PAF is published by The Church of Jesus Christ of Latter-day Saints, and is available to anyone at the low cost of $15 from LDS Church Distribution Centers. The address of the Salt Lake Distribution Center is 1999 West 1700 South, Salt Lake City, Utah 84104. The current version for the MS-DOS (IBM and compatible) is 3.0; for Macintosh, version 2.31. Illustrations in this publication use the MS Dos 3.0 version. The Personal Ancestral File software can be used to submit names for Ancestral File or Names Clearance to the LDS Church. While a DOS application, PAF works well with Windows and Windows 95. (*See also* Personal Ancestral File Companion.)

PAF User Groups

Several user groups have developed across the country, with users helping each other in learning to make better use of Personal Ancestral File, as well as in programming add-on utilities to enhance its functionality. Some groups have contacted the Family History Department Support Group in Salt Lake City and provide help under their guidance. The local groups also serve to provide input for future versions of Personal Ancestral File and as testers for software enhancements and changes. For a list of user groups in your area, write to:

Personal Ancestral File
50 East North Temple Street
Salt Lake City, UT 84150

Personal Ancestral File® Companion

A software program published by the LDS Church that allows one to print quality copies of family group records, pedigree charts and other reports using data in your Personal Ancestral File genealogy data base, if using version 3.0. It is a Windows program, while PAF 3.0 is a DOS program. It is available for $10.00 from the LDS Church Distribution Center.

Personal history

The history of one person. Even though a personal history may refer to other family members, they are incidental to the life of the person whose history is being written.

Places

A specific location, determined by a civil or ecclesiastical description, such as a town, county, state, country, or a church congregation (parish, or LDS ward or stake).

Places are normally listed beginning with the smallest level. (Example: parish, town, county, state or country, as Tryon, Polk, NC).

When looking for records about your ancestors, look at all levels (jurisdictions) that may have created records, such as churches, cemeteries, towns or cities, counties, townships, states, regions, provinces, countries, etc.

Place levels are separated by commas, such as Salt Lake City, Salt Lake, Utah. If you do not know the county, you can leave a blank space and insert an additional comma, as Salt Lake City, , Utah; or Salt Lake City,,Utah. If you know a county, but don't know a town or there was no town (the event happened in the country), write out the word *county* or abbreviate it, as Salt Lake County, Utah; or Salt Lake Co., Utah. Or you can place a comma in front of the name of the county: ,Greene, Iowa.

"Of" places. When the exact place of an event is not known, use a place where the person or a member of his or her family are known to have lived (often called a place of residence). Use the word "of" in front of the place name: "of Tryon, Polk, NC."

Postal guides are good references to help determine the county for any town in the United States, and old ones can often be purchased inexpensively. Gazetteers also usually give this information.

Changes often occur in the jurisdiction of a place. When looking for records that pertain to your family, look under all places (jurisdictions) that the locality has been a part of. For example, if a town was originally located in Orange County, NC, but later Caswell County was created from Orange County and the town was then located in Caswell County, both Orange and Caswell county records may contain records of your family.

Places often changed boundaries during the development of an area. Understanding these changes is necessary to know where to look for records of your ancestors during a certain time period. For the United States, an excellent source that traces the development of counties is *The Handy Book for Genealogists* (Logan, Utah: Everton Publishers).

Names of places often change, as well as boundaries. It is helpful to show the place as it was named at the time of the event, followed in parentheses by its name as it presently is known, as Orange (now Caswell) County, NC.

This problem can cause different types of complications. For example, if the town was originally Bradford and was annexed into Haverhill, you can find authentic records that tell you a person was born in Bradford, and also that say he/she was born in Haverhill. It still may be the same person, and both records may be correct. But if you need to find the records, you may have to look in Haverhill, even though it was called Bradford when the event occurred. But if the place divided, and part is now called Bradford and part is called Haverhill, then either or both places may have the early records.

Primary sources

Sources that were created at the time of the event, by someone who knew. A birth certificate is a primary source. A death certificate (or vital record of that event kept by anyone, created at the time of the event) is a primary source for the death information, but is a secondary source for the birth information and names of parents.

Printout

A paper copy of a report from a computer. For example, pedigree charts or family group records printed from Ancestral File are printouts.

Also, a term used in the IGI to refer to an alphabetical list of all names extracted from a specific town or church (or group of such records, as all christenings in Manchester Cathedral in England for about 300 years) that can be viewed on microfiche or microfilm.

Probate records

A will and/or other documents associated with the settling of the estate of a deceased person. It usually includes a list of the heirs, with the relationship of each to the deceased.

Proof

Two meanings: (1) To carefully read and re-read something to make sure that it does not contain errors; (2) that which causes the mind to accept something as fact.

Research Calendar

A record of your research activity — past, present, and future. It should include your research goal or objective (what you are looking for), and the records you want to search — by description and library call number. Then as you search each record, add comments about what you found (or did not find) and cross-references to more details notes and documents. It thus becomes the history of your research.

Research goal

Information you wish to find. Your goal will determine the sources you will look in. You should always identify your research goals, and plan your searches around completing them, one by one. Examples of goals (sometimes called objectives): find the birth date of Grandpa John A. Stevens; find the marriage record for Aunt Veva; find out how many children Grandpa Harry Nichols had; find when the family moved from Maine to Massachusetts, or from Massachusetts to Wisconsin.

Research process

A series of steps to follow in pursuing a research objective. Various versions of these steps are in print. One is a five-step approach: one, identify what you already know about your family (or about this particular ancestor); two, determine what you want to learn about them; three, identify and select a record to search; four, obtain and search the record; five, evaluate and use the results (which includes recording it and its source citation). The process is then repeated. This version expects you to include recording your information and sources as part of the other steps. Some versions identify these tasks as separate steps.

RIN

In the Personal Ancestral File (PAF), a record identification number.

Royalty and medieval records

Records for families of kings (royalty) and for persons born earlier than 1500 (medieval). This includes legitimate and illegitimate offspring.

The Genealogical Society of Utah/Family History Library had a special unit that directed the compilation of these and many other affiliated records, using volunteers. Many of these records have been added to Ancestral File. Because of the complexity of understanding these records, there are some limitations on what can be done with records for this time period in submitting them to FamilySearch files. Contact the Family History Department for more details. Before you consider submitting to Ancestral File any records on persons who may be considered part of royal families or were born pre-1500, please check Ancestral File to see if the records are already there. You may need to search under a number of possible names and spellings.

The names of royalty may be listed differently from what you expect to find in Ancestral File and in the International Genealogical Index. For detail see under "Royalty and Medieval Records" in the publication *Genealogy in the Computer Age: Understanding FamilySearch®*, volume 1, by Elizabeth L. Nichols.

Sealed

An LDS term referring to binding families together for eternity. *See also* Ordinances.

Secondary sources

Records that were made long after the event occurred or were compiled from other records.

Sibling

Brother or sister.

Source

Where something came from; for example, the source of your own birth date may be personal knowledge; or a source may be a birth certificate or a printed family history. Source citations usually include enough detail so someone else can locate the record.

Source citation

The way a source is referenced or described.

SourceGuide™

A computerized file using Folio to provide how-to information about family history sources allowing one to benefit from the knowledge and experience of experts in the field. Published on compact disc by The Church of Jesus Christ of Latter-day Saints; available for home use by anyone; cost 1998 is $20.00. (See also page 42.)

Spouse

A wife or husband.

TempleReady™

A program for members of The Church of Jesus Christ of Latter-day Saints, for submitting names for temple ordinances. It is part of FamilySearch.

Time Line

A chart that shows in a graphic manner the events in a person's life from birth until present or from birth until death. A horizontal (straight) line represents one's life. Vertical lines represent events. The distance between the vertical lines help show the time span between events. It can be as detailed or limited as desired.

Tradition

The delivery of opinions, doctrines, practices, rites, and customs from generation to generation by oral communication; also, a long- established custom or practice that has the effect of an unwritten law"; also stories within the family about their origin or about a specific ancestor.

Transcribed

A written copy; for example, a transcribed copy of a birth record from the 1850s means that someone has deciphered the letters and decided what the name was, and written it down. *See also* Original.

U.S. Social Security Death Index

An index of names with brief details of persons who had Social Security numbers and whose deaths were reported to the Social Security office between the years of 1962-1988 (with a few earlier and later). It is made available by the U.S. Government Freedom of Information Act.

The LDS Church has purchased tapes of the information and makes the information available to the public as part of FamilySearch.

Upload

Taking automated records that have been downloaded (copied) from one computerized file and adding them to another computer file without retyping the information.

Version

Similar to edition, it is used with software. For example, Personal Ancestral File 3.0 means this is a version identified as 3.0, which is different (has additional features and functions) from version 2.31, or 2.1 or 2.0.

Vital records

Records that were created for the purpose of recording births, marriages, and deaths, or christenings, weddings and burials. The term is used more in the United States and Canada, while civil registration and other terms may be used in other cultures.

INDEX

See also the glossary, pages 63-77
Action 6, 8, 10, 11, 17, 31
Address
    of Family History Educators (*see* copyright page)
    of major genealogical organizations 31
Ancestor 5, 63
Ancestral File 44, 62, 63
Backup 63
Basics 5, 7, 8, 39, 50
Begin 5, 10, 39, 50
Calendar of Events 17, 63
Census records 14, 64
Compact disc 27, 43, 65
Computers 26, 39, 65
    and genealogy 39
    equipment 39, 49
    hardware 40, 65
    helps 59
    learning about 39
    Internet 47
    software 40, 50, 65
    using to find genealogical information 41
    using to organize and record information 49
    using to share information 61
    when you have never used one before 39
Dates 8, 65
Definitions 63
Discrepancy chart 18
Document file 17
Electronic Media 47
E-mail 47
Family 5
    group record explanation 6, 7, 8, 9, 37
    forms 6, 22, 34, 35
    blended 9
    heritage 29
FamilySearch 44, 68
Forms
    address for free catalog 8
    blank ones 32-35
    completed ones 36-37
    calendar of events 17
    discrepancy chart 18
    family group record 6, 7, 8, 22, 34, 35, 37
    formats vary 8, 26, 34, 35, 37
    how to fill out 9

LDS 22, 35
    pedigree chart 5, 7, 8, 20, 32, 33, 36
    research calendar 16
GEDCOM 27, 44, 46, 61, 69
Given names 5
Home sources 6, 11
Identifying persons – four parts of, 5
Information
    evaluating 15, 18
    how to find 6, 10, 41
    how to organize 7, 49
    how to share 44, 61
    where to get 6, 10, 13, 14, 15, 41
International Genealogical Index (IGI) 44, 71
Internet
    introduction to 47
    newsgroups 49
    places to visit 48
    search engines 49
LDS helps 22
    computer software programs 23, 26, 27
    duplicate checking 25, 26
    forms 22, 33, 35
    LDS options 47
    ordinances 22, 23, 25, 26, 33, 35, 73
TempleReady 23, 25, 77
    what is different 22
Letter-writing helps 11, 12
Libraries, major 31
Maiden name 5
Microfilm 13, 15, 72
Names 5, 8, 18, 19, 72
Original sources 73
Pedigree 5, 7, 27, 32, 33, 36, 53, 56
Personal Ancestral File (PAF) 24, 26, 27, 50, 74
Personal Ancestral File Companion 28, 39, 75
Personal knowledge as a source 6, 10, 25
Photographs (pictures) 27
Places 5, 8, 51, 56, 75
Primary sources 75
Print 29, 48, 56
Research goals 16, 76
Research calendar 16, 76
Research process 76
Research help (*see* SourceGuide)
Software 40, 50, 65
Secondary sources 76

ources 6, 10, 11, 12, 21, 42, 48, 57, 76
   beyond personal knowledge 10
   census 14
   certificates 13
   compiled 14
   home 6, 11
   original 73
   personal knowledge 6, 10
   primary 75
   transcribed 77
   recording 20, 57, 77
   secondary 76
   vital records 13
ourceGuide™ 42, 77
urname 5
empleReady 47, 77 (*see also* 25, 26, 27, 47, 62)
ital records 13
Web sites 48

ABOUT THE AUTHOR:

Elizabeth L. Nichols is well known as an author and teacher in the field of genealogy and family history. She is an accredited genealogist (A.G.) by the Family History Library of The Church of Jesus Christ of Latter-day Saints (Mormons). She was the primary writer on the Boy Scouts of America merit badge pamphlet for genealogy, 1988 edition. A long-time employee of a large genealogy/family history organization, Elizabeth has worked with large and small databases since 1973 and with computer programs since 1981.

She is listed in *Who's Who in Genealogy and Heraldry* and other similar publications. The *Genesis of Your Genealogy*, her first book, first published in 1969 and totally revised and updated, remains a popular help for individuals who wish to trace their own families and for teachers who wish to help others.

Other books and pamphlets by Elizabeth L. Nichols include:

Genealogy in the Computer Age: Understanding FamilySearch®, volumes 1 and 2

> *Volume 1: Ancestral File, International Genealogical Index (IGI), Social Security Death Index*, revised edition 1994, 56 pages, 60 illustrations

> *Volume 2: Family History Library Catalog, More Resource Files, Personal Ancestral File, and Using Them All in Harmony,* includes case studies and step-by-step guidelines and pitfalls to avoid. 1997, 88 pages, 86 illustrations

Finding Your Relationship to a Known Relative (6 pages)

Teaching Family Heritage in Four Weeks: A Course Outline (10 pages)

Her articles have been published by various genealogical periodicals or newsletters, such as a series of seven articles explaining the International Genealogical Index published by the Federation of Genealogical Societies in the *FGS Forum, 1993-1998.*

WOULD YOU LIKE TO KNOW. . . ?

(This publication answers these questions and more!)

1. What do I need to know to begin my genealogy? (See page 5.)
2. What form do I use to record the complete family unit? (See page 8.)
3. What is a pedigree chart? (See page 7.)
4. Where do I get the information? (See page 6.)
5. What is oral genealogy? (See page 6.)
6. What are home sources? (See pages 6, 11.)
7. How do I record the information when all my children are not from the same marriage? (See page 9.)
8. What do I do when I have recorded all that my family and I already know? (See page 10.)
9. What are compiled records? (See page 14.)
10. What are original records? (See page 70.)
11. What are vital records? (See page 13.)
12. What are primary records? (See page 72.)
13. What might census records contain about my family? (See page 14.)
14. Where may I find these records? (See pages 12, 14.)
15. What is evidence and how do I use it? (See pages 19, 64.)
16. What is a research calendar? (See page 16.)
17. What is a calendar of events? (See page 17.)
18. What is a document file? (See page 17.)
19. What is a discrepancy chart? (See page 18.)
20. What should I include when I list my sources? (See pages 20.)
21. What is different for the LDS family historian? (See page 22.)
22. What is a Time Line? (See page 28.)
23. What is the address for the National Archive Regional center nearest me? (See page 31.)
24. What if I have never used a computer? (See page 39.)
25. What is computer hardware? (See pages 40, 65.)
26. What is computer software? (See pages 40, 50, 65.)
27. How might I use the computer to find family history information? (See page 41.)
28. How might I use the computer to organize and record information? (See page 49.)
29. How might I use the computer to share genealogy information? (See page 61.)
30. What is FamilySearch? (See pages 44, 68.)
31. How does FamilySearch work? (See page 45.)
32. What can I expect a genealogy software program to do for me? (See page 50.)
33. Where can I find the definition of terms that everyone is using? (See pages 63-77.)
34. How do I DO my family history? (See ACTION, pages 6, 8, 10, 11, 17, 31.)
35. How do I submit my family records to Ancestral File? (See page 62.)
36. What is "e-mail"? (See page 47.)
37. Can the Internet help me with family history? (See page 47.)
38. Can I include pictures? (See page 27.)